The Art of Coaching

The Art of Coaching is a book to shift thinking and open up new possibilities, to stimulate fresh insight, to adapt to your needs as a coach or manager and to use creatively in practice. Written by two experienced, highly qualified international coaches and supervisors, this creative book offers ideas to use across the range of coaching contexts including leadership, decision making, change and supervision.

Combining brand-new, original diagrams with classic models from the learning development and management fields, Jenny Bird and Sarah Gornall have created a valuable resource for quick reference, instant accessibility and fast learning, built on a strong theoretical base. Each model in the book is explained with a clear, accessible diagram and a simple guide to what it is, how it works and how to put it into action. The text is full of inspiration for applications of the ideas in scenarios based on real coaching practice.

The Art of Coaching will be an invaluable companion for coaches looking for new ways of developing awareness with clients, coaching students and trainees, coach supervisors, Learning and Development professionals and those working in Human Resource departments.

Jenny Bird has successfully coached CEOs, senior executives and other leaders since 2000. She supervises coaches internationally to develop their competence and enhance their coaching presence. She has been in the forefront of the development of coaching in the UK and is in demand as a speaker at conferences nationally and internationally.

Sarah Gornall is a coach, mentor, supervisor and trainer. She works with coaches across the UK and internationally to develop coaching competence and confidence, and coaches leaders and managers across the private, public and not-for-profit sectors. The author of two previous books, her wide experience informs her creative approach to supporting great professional coaching.

The Art of Coaching

A Handbook of Tips and Tools

Jenny Bird and
Sarah Gornall

Routledge
Taylor & Francis Group

LONDON AND NEW YORK

First published 2016
by Routledge
2 Park Square, Milton Park, Abingdon, Oxon, OX14 4RN

and by Routledge
711 Third Avenue, New York, NY 10017

Routledge is an imprint of the Taylor & Francis Group, an informa business

© 2016 Jenny Bird and Sarah Gornall

The right of Jenny Bird and Sarah Gornall to be identified as authors of this work has been asserted by them in accordance with sections 77 and 78 of the Copyright, Designs and Patents Act 1988.

British Library Cataloguing in Publication Data
A catalogue record for this book is available from the British Library

Library of Congress Cataloging in Publication Data
  Bird, Jenny.
  The art of coaching: a handbook of tips and tools/Jenny Bird and
  Sarah Gornall. – 1 Edition.
  pages cm
  Includes bibliographical references and index.
  1. Personal coaching. I. Gornall, Sarah. II. Title.
  BF637.P36B53 2015
  158.3–dc23
  2015010187

ISBN: 978-1-138-89185-2 (hbk)
ISBN: 978-1-138-89186-9 (pbk)
ISBN: 978-1-315-70947-5 (ebk)

Typeset in Frutiger
by Florence Production Ltd, Stoodleigh, Devon, UK

Contents

Acknowledgements   vii
About the authors and illustrator   ix

1   **Introduction**   1

2   **Coaching**   11

3   **Relationships and Communication**   37

4   **Learning and Personal Growth**   67

5   **Leading, Influencing and Motivating**   95

6   **Analysis, Choice and Change**   123

7   **Supervision and Team Facilitation**   157

8   **Developing Creativity**   185

9   **References and Further Reading**   205

Index   225

Acknowledgements

First we want to thank the support team: Dennis, Martin, Rachel, Alison, Ros, Steve, Gwyn and Dennis.

You can all now stop saying '*I thought you had finished the book*'. Because we have! And we know Dennis is on the list twice: that's for all the tea, cake and ice cream to succour us.

We are grateful to all the colleagues and clients who have encouraged us along the way: Jo Birch, Vivienne Bolton, Saima Butt, Rob Goode, Erik de Haan, Barum Jeffries, Pat Marum, Trudi Newton, Moira Palmer, Helen Seiroda (of Wise Goose), Penny de Valk, James Walker, Liz Wiggins and Lindsay Wittenberg. The Gritty Girls were there at the beginning and cheered us on to the end.

We are also grateful to the following for permission to redraw and describe copyright material: Robert Dilts for his own work on Neurological Levels; Trudi Newton for her work on the Supervision Triangle; the Taylor & Francis Group for Bruce Peltier's drawing of the Johari Window; SAGE for Sarah Gornall's drawings of the Developmental Wheel and Review Pentagon; the Society of Friends for the two mules diagram; and the creative clients whose work we share in Chapter 8.

We must also acknowledge Josie Vallely for her stalwart work on the illustrations. She has found the balance between staying with our ideas and adding something original to bring them to life on the page.

About the authors and illustrator

Jenny Bird is an acclaimed executive coach, working with senior leaders since 2000, a coach supervisor and mentor. She is passionate about building a profession of competent and accredited coaches and is known internationally for her contributions to coaching standards and professionalism. A graduate of the University of Oxford, Jenny worked for many years in adult and community education with special dedication to higher education for non-traditional students. She has been a speaker and facilitator at numerous masterclasses, webinars and conferences for coaches across the world. Read more about Jenny at: www.coachsupervisor.co.uk

Sarah Gornall is an established coach, supervisor, mentor and trainer, highly respected for her contributions to the coaching profession in the UK and to the development of coaching skills in education. She works with business leaders and coaches across the UK and internationally. A graduate of the University of Cambridge, she has over 30 years' experience in Learning and Development. Previous books include *Coaching and Learning in Schools: A Practical Guide*. Sarah has been a board member of several not-for-profit organisations, including the UK ICF (International Coach Federation). Read more about Sarah at: www.coachingclimate.co.uk

Together, their insights, models and methods support great coaching practice internationally. They are committed to the use of coaching principles to promote collaborative environments for human endeavour in business, public service and personal relationships.

Josie Vallely is an illustrator based in Scotland. She graduated from Glasgow School of Art with a Master's of Illustration in 2014, and has since worked with a wide range of clients, including Routledge, HarperCollins, RSPB, Woodcraft Folk UK, Historic Scotland, Creative Edinburgh and Glasgow School of Art. Explore her portfolio at: www.josievallely.com

Chapter 1

Introduction

Who is this book for?

Why did we write it?

What would you like to get out of it?

About the Book

Diagrams, maps, symbols, signs and models cut through complexity with clarity and immediacy. That is why *The Art of Coaching* is a book of drawings.

The way coaching is often taught, as a process of conversation, dialogue and words, appeals to the auditory and reflective thinker. We hope this book, with its constant interplay of words and images, will stimulate visual thinking and will prompt creative and versatile ways of working to connect with clients at a deeper level.

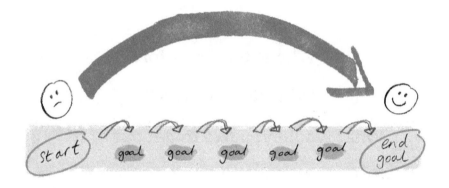

Here, we use diagrams to explain our thinking and fast-track understanding of concepts and models. We describe how we use drawing ourselves and give you some tips for how you might do so too. We hope this will help you make well-known models your own, understand people better and explore new ways of representing ideas.

The Art of Coaching comes out of our own experience. Both of us are experienced coaches, trainers, and coach supervisors and mentors. We have served our time as managers and employers.

We have discovered that when we use drawing and diagrams with our clients, they grasp complex ideas quickly, unravel their thinking and are able to move on from places where they have been stuck. Creating sketches together can be revelatory, leading to new perspectives and shifts in thinking.

In fast-moving business environments, people want to be able to grasp complex ideas quickly and to apply them to their situation now.

Relationship is at the heart of coaching. As we listen to a client, our connection and synergy grow. The more we use all our senses to communicate, the deeper the connection and the more powerful the work. Using diagrams sometimes enables us to go to places where words would not take us. This will not suit every client on every occasion. Connect first; then choose how to work.

We hope this book will give you:

*   ideas
*   new thinking
*   practical models
*   ways to stimulate creative dialogue with clients
*   activities to suit different learning styles.

We aim to develop practice rather than theory. While many of the models are based on research, we leave you to follow up ideas that interest you and to explore them in more depth, using the references at the end of the book.

By the end of the book, we hope you will have a more varied toolkit on which to draw, and a greater ability to help others with different ways of seeing the world so they can unlock their thinking and move forward.

Our experience of using drawing

Here's an example of what happened in a recent coaching session. A client arrived with an iPad. Faced with the company's pro forma on which to draft coaching objectives, he declared, '*I don't do paper. I use my iPad for everything.*' A few minutes into the session, the coach asked, '*So what's this for? What's the bigger picture?*' '*Can I borrow a pen?*' the client responded. '*I'll draw a diagram.*' Talking about the diagram and its implications, linked processes and hidden layers, stimulated new perspectives.

He left the session lighter in mind, with a plan of action, new ways of seeing the issue – and seven sheets of self-generated diagrams and handwritten prompts.

Coaching is a partnership that stimulates thinking and new perspectives, so we want to work in a way that helps this to happen more often. When a client sits down with an iPad and starts tapping in everything either of us says, our antennae quiver, for we have noticed that this often leads to a focus on the mechanics of data entry rather than a creative flow of ideas. We find that this can stultify rather than stimulate thinking, and may capture exploratory comments and fix them as absolute truths, shutting down the mind rather than opening it up.

It's quite different when one of us picks up a pen or pencil to start drawing a diagram. It's as though the thinking process is externalised. We can both engage with the diagram and ask questions about it. We can talk about the sequence of a process, overlapping responsibilities, blurred boundaries, tensions between opposing forces, pressure from different sources. With the diagram out there before us, some of the heat is taken out of the issue. It's objectivised. The two of us can sit together and take an external view of it. We can ask, '*How come it's like that?*' provoking an objective discussion, where the client is able to deal with difficult material without feeling personally challenged. We can ask, '*Is this how you'd like it to look?*' and '*What would you prefer?*'

Elements of the diagram are both memory hooks and shortcuts. Clients can point to something and say '*this*' instead of repeatedly describing a process or finding an apt word. As they point at or touch the diagram, they think about what lies behind '*this*', impacts on '*this*' or connects with '*this*'. Together, we can build up visual layers or maps that explain the complexity of a situation – and when several layers or elements have been added, the relationship of each to the other and of each to the whole becomes apparent. Writing on one part of the diagram releases the mind from the burden of remembering so it's easier to bring focus and energy to the next piece of the jigsaw.

Recent research into how the mind holds and deals with information seems to fit with conclusions we have drawn from own experiments. David Rock, the founder of the NeuroLeadership Institute, writes in *Your Brain at Work* that using visuals reduces the energy needed for processing information and therefore maximises the energy left for thinking and performing. He tells us that pictures use the visual cortex in the occipital lobe, at the back of the brain. This frees up more space in the prefrontal cortex for higher-level thinking tasks and understanding complex ideas.

Both of us have coaching clients who initiate drawings. '*Do you mind if I show you . . .*' they might say, or '*It looks like this.*'

Both of us initiate drawing ourselves in response to a client's words or description. '*I've been getting a picture of where you are*' we might say, or '*What I'm seeing is this . . . is it all right if I sketch it out?*'

Both of us at times alternate drawing with our clients, who sometimes almost seize the pen from our grasp and take control of the image for themselves.

Our supervision clients also describe similar experiences to us. We conclude that using drawing and diagrams is relatively common and adds an extra dimension to our work, increasing the chances of breakthrough moments.

In all this work, the aim is to expand the client's perceptions. We want to stress how vital it is that the drawing of a situation, process or model is a support or expansion of the client's agenda. When we offer to sketch something, it is:

- stimulated by what the client is exploring
- offered without attachment
- *not* the coach's choice or agenda
- optional – the client could say '*No*'
- ultimately owned by the client.

We and the client collaborate on creating a model that is relevant and unique to the client. It goes beyond both the client's original thinking and the original model that we may have introduced.

How the book is organised

The book focuses in turn on different themes, each illustrated by a series of shapes, diagrams and pictures. Some of the models are well known and widely used in the business world, for organisational development and team building, for analysis and coaching. Others are our own original creations, generated in the course of coaching, training or supervising.

In all instances, the diagram or shape we offer is not a fixed truth or definitive explanation of a situation or relationship. Its value lies in the sense the client makes of it. Drawing and reflecting on models in the moment stimulates new insights into both individuals and organisations. It is not the theory that matters so much as the light and energy that the model generates.

The book is organised around the following themes:

- coaching
- relationships and communication
- learning and personal growth
- leading, influencing and motivating
- analysis, choice and change
- supervision and team facilitation
- developing creativity.

The layout of most of the book looks like this

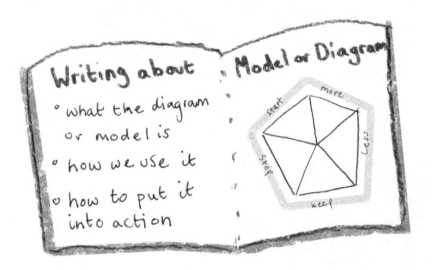

We explain the idea or model behind each picture or diagram and how we might use it, then suggest questions or approaches to help you take this idea into your own practice. We have kept the writing concise, without spelling out what you might do in huge detail, hoping to prompt you to think about how to use the models for yourself.

We finish off with a bibliography of references where we have mentioned other published works in our text. It offers you the opportunity of following up in more depth on theory and research if you would like to do so.

How might you use the book?

Be creative. You can use all the models in a variety of situations. Please be bold. Many of these models have already been extended and developed by others before you. So adapt them according to your circumstances, the context in which you are working and the inspiration of the moment.

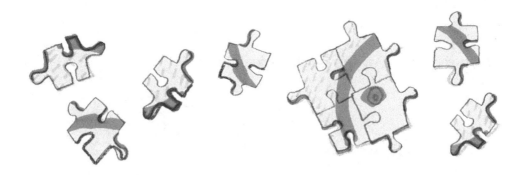

The value of this book is in how you make it your own. Our explanations are deliberately light touch. We aim to:
*   stimulate thinking
*   remind you of well-known models
*   inspire you to be creative
*   stretch your practice
*   pique your interest to explore more
*   point you to further reading.

Like any idea, this book, once out of our minds, can be used in whatever way you, the reader, wish, with the usual exceptions of plagiarism, mass photocopying and presentation as your own work.

Coaching is often described in terms of words and the silence between them. Great coaches create awareness through deep listening and insightful questioning. Our experience has led us to think that we also create awareness through imagery and the visual world. And while our diagrams are, in a sense, statements made by us or other people, we hope they will not remain trapped on the page, but will spring to life as you and the people you coach grab a pen or pencil and interact with each other and your interpretation of what you see.

We hope you will carry this book around with you, read it in gaps between interactions, meetings and sessions, and dip into it for fun and inspiration; in short, anything other than reading it to send you to sleep at night.

And we'd be interested to hear about where it has taken you. Who knows where that dialogue might lead?

It is your choice how you work with this book. You might get indigestion if you take on too much in one go. Bite-sized chunks might be both easier to absorb and much more fun.

Chapter 2

Coaching

Coaching

This chapter focuses on the enterprise of coaching: the shape of the contract, coaching interactions and stakeholder maps. We start from the assumption that you, the reader, already have an understanding of the skills and processes of coaching. Other books offer an excellent introduction to how to coach, though no book will actually teach anyone as well as a live professional training programme with demonstration and practice. Here, we offer something additional that we hope will help you extend your reflection and practice.

As coaches, we are accustomed to using models and diagrams to understand and configure our clients' worlds and psychological processes. We use them both during our own professional training and in our practice with clients to understand their thinking and processing. It is much rarer to use diagrams to explain the process of coaching itself. This is what we set out to do here.

We stand back from the process to gain a different perspective – one that helps us to reflect on what we are doing and how we are doing it. We articulate and interpret the relational space in which we work.

As elsewhere in the book, we illustrate our thinking and provide stimulus for yours through visual diagrams. All the models in this chapter are original to us. They have evolved through years of coaching experience.

We start by thinking about the process of coaching, the focus of the work and the interaction between two people in one session and over time. Then we look at the many factors that influence the interaction: our own learning, personal and professional contexts, as well as the clients' organisational, systemic and psychological contexts.

When we were first coaching, we often had to answer the question, '*Which sport?*' That question is rarer now. Over time, we have watched the professional space and scope of coaching develop and become more mainstream, so today it is understood, accepted by and used in many businesses, government departments, and public-sector and not-for-profit organisations. The context defines the system in which the professional relationship is set. It is often complex, with numerous dimensions and stakeholders. The 'coachee' may be a team of people. The organisation and the commissioning sponsor are clients who are often unseen but nevertheless a present influence on the interaction between coach and client. As a result, there is a need for layered contracting and careful definitions of the work. Our models illustrate this.

We believe that coaching is a practical strategy that helps someone achieve outcomes they identify themselves. The outcomes may be about perceptions and beliefs as well as about observable behaviour and concrete action. Coaching leads to insight, discovery and forward movement, in alignment with the uniqueness of the individual, their understanding of the world, values and preferences. Relationship is the foundation of its success.

The Coaching Process

What this is

Coaching is a learning activity with its own cycle of action, reflection, shifting awareness and reapplication.

The client takes action outside the coaching space. She (or he) comes out of their normal context into relationship with the coach for a brief period and then returns to their world, of which we are not generally part. The short time we are together has to be rich to stimulate new insights and changed behaviours. So it's important that we understand what goes on.

Coaching allows the client to reflect on the action and how it is impacted by other elements of their world – personal, systemic, physical, emotional, evidenced and assumed; to identify key issues and underlying motivations; to create new ways of telling their story; to think differently; to apply their changed perceptions in planning and rehearsing alternative behaviours.

How we use it

Different coaching approaches are particularly appropriate at different stages in the process. We use this diagram to reflect on our practice with clients, or to prompt reflection with supervisees, asking:

- *Where was the client at ease/not at ease/stuck?*
- *Was there a stage in the process that was missing/incomplete?*
- *What might the coach have done differently at certain stages?*
- *How was the dance between the client and the coach?*

Put it into action

Use this diagram to:

- reflect on your own practice
- explain the developmental process to potential buyers of coaching
- support participants on training courses
- check that you allow enough time for each stage of the process when you are working with or developing a team.

The Coaching Process

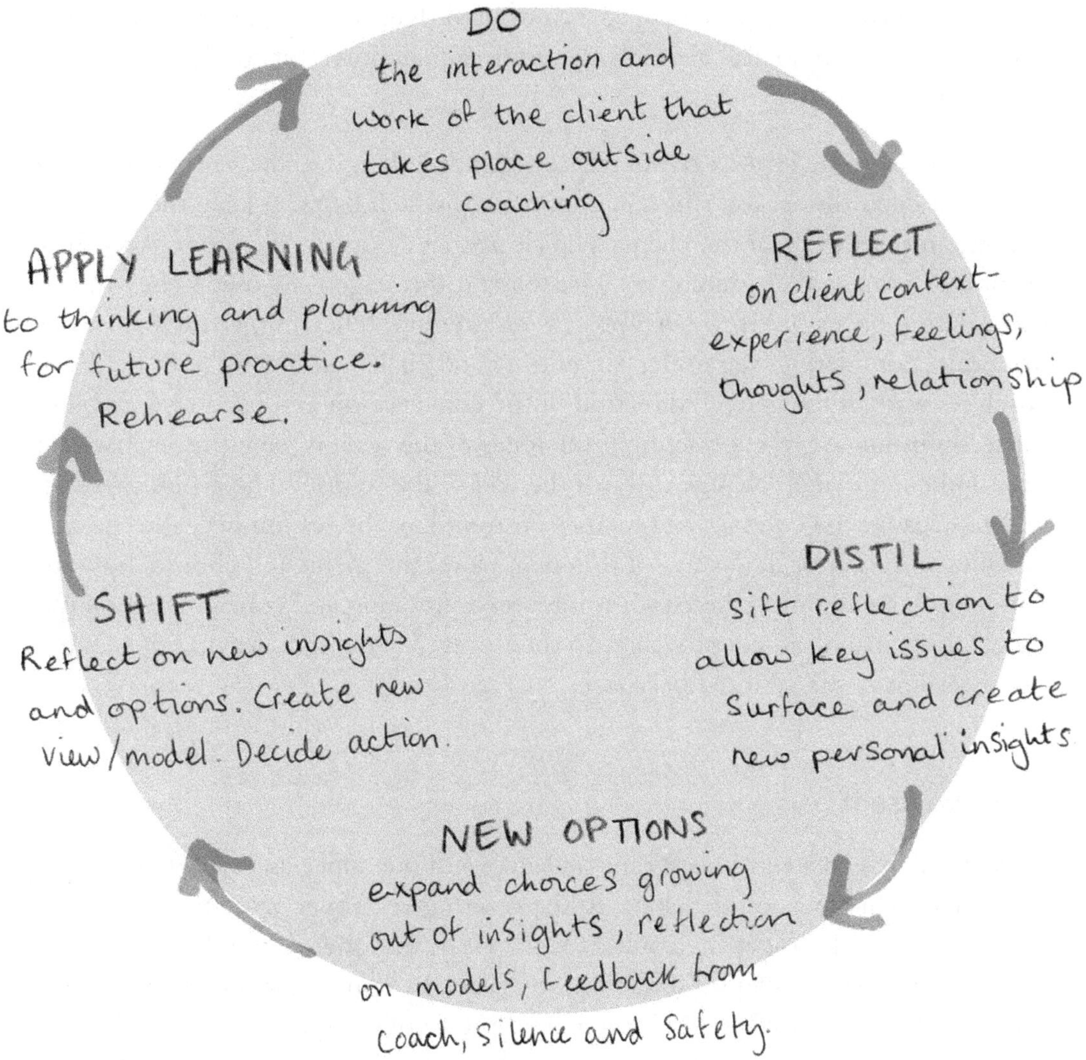

DO
the interaction and
work of the client that
takes place outside
coaching

APPLY LEARNING
to thinking and planning
for future practice.
Rehearse.

REFLECT
on client context-
experience, feelings,
thoughts, relationship

SHIFT
Reflect on new insights
and options. Create new
view/model. Decide action.

DISTIL
Sift reflection to
allow key issues to
surface and create
new personal insights

NEW OPTIONS
expand choices growing
out of insights, reflection
on models, feedback from
coach, silence and safety.

A Coaching Session

What this is

This diagram tells us something about the shape of a typical coaching session.

The coach arrives at the coaching space prepared. Reflection helps to create the presence and psychological alertness that underpin all powerful coaching experiences.

There may be some chat to create relationship, and then the focus narrows. Coach and client enter the session through contracting, which helps to keep the work safe and in the service of the client. The clearer the contract, the more likely the client is to achieve their outcomes. The work at this stage is focused. Then the conversation opens out through a process of listening, reflecting, clarifying, exploring, considering, reframing, supporting and challenging. All the time, the coach is aware of the general direction of the conversation and has a responsibility for reconfirming or re-contracting if the focus of the session seems to be changing. Pace and energy often change towards the end of the session. The coach checks progress against the contract and focuses on rounding the session off. The client commits to action or new ways of thinking, closes the menu and chooses how to go forward. At all times, the coach is interested, listening and concentrated on the client. Both coach and client walk into their everyday context, leaving the content of the session in the confidential space.

How we use it

This image was created to clarify for ourselves and our supervisees how an effective coaching session develops. It helps us to give proper value to different stages of our work, to get the contract really clear, to notice when the conversation takes a different direction, to revisit the contract and to review the session in the light of what was agreed. The nature of the questions often changes as we round off the session, when we might be more forceful in testing out the client's commitment and strategies for overcoming potential saboteurs of their good intentions.

A Coaching Session

Put it into action

Periodically, check your sessions contain all these elements by:

• listening to a recording (made with prior permission, of course)
• discussing with a supervisor
• reflecting systematically through each element.

In the moment with a client, ask yourself where you are and where you need to be next.

Sticking With the Contract

What this is

We sketched out this diagram with a client who was talking about his problems with a subcontractor. They started off with a clear contract for a limited amount of work. The project went well. The subcontractor delivered. The client asked for more work, and more again. As time went by, the work that the subcontractor was doing diverged more and more from the core contract and quality went down. He didn't have the skills or personnel to deliver. There was no review built into the system. People had been going down new avenues without looking at the fit with the original contract. Everyone was too busy getting on with the job to see what was happening until things went really wrong. Analysis of the problem and corrective action took longer because it came at a late stage.

How we use it

We use this diagram in more than one way. We:
*   remind ourselves of the danger of drifting away from what we have agreed with a client, for a session or for a series
*   look at it with a client in relation to a problem they are describing, asking questions such as *'What was the original agreement?'*, *'How did you make that clear?'*, *'How did that work?'*, *'Where are you now on this diagram?'*, *'So what could you do?'*, and *'What's the learning?'*
*   consider it with supervisees in relation to their practice.

Sometimes we draw the diagram with a completely horizontal core, sometimes diverging from the original trajectory a bit. That's life. Both projects and coaching sessions may legitimately move away from the original specification or contract. The point is that we need to check with the client that this is in their service, and to agree the changed intention or outcomes before we proceed.

Put it into action

In reflection on your own practice, or your situation at work, ask yourself:
*   *What was the contract?*
*   *Who owned it? How much?*
*   *Where are we now? How close to/far from the original agreement?*
*   *What might need to happen next?*
*   *How can I build regular reviews into my work?*

Sticking With the Contract

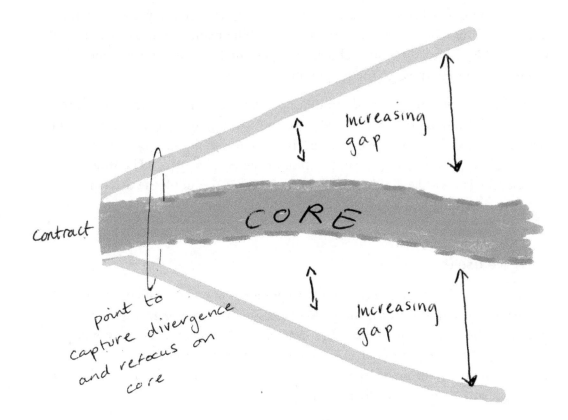

A Coaching Series

What this is

Sometimes clients come to coaching with huge goals. They have no idea how they are going to achieve the outcome they desire, because it represents such a huge shift from where they are at the moment. The overarching arrow represents this shift. Describing this end goal helps to keep the coaching on track and gives momentum and purpose to the programme.

A coaching series is made up of a number of sessions, each of which has its own goal, or desired outcome. These goals serve as stepping stones towards the overall outcome. This process is represented in the diagram by the smaller ovals and arrows, all heading in the general direction of the end outcome. The smiley represents client satisfaction by the end of the series. We think the diagram says this better than the words!

How we use it

We have used this diagram primarily with potential purchasers of coaching, both organisational and individual, and participants on coach training. It is very effective when used as an animated PowerPoint slide where the starting block and the end goal appear first on a blank screen, then the overarching arrow representing the shift or the leap to be made, then the series of goals and smaller steps, one at a time, and finally the smiley.

The diagram is also helpful when talking about the review process in coaching. It is our responsibility as coaches to help clients to keep on track and, if they do decide to change where they are heading, to ensure that this is consciously surfaced and that the contract is renewed and adjusted explicitly.

We may use the diagram with supervisees or mentees as food for the discussion about how they are holding their clients accountable and supporting progress towards their desired outcomes.

A Coaching Series

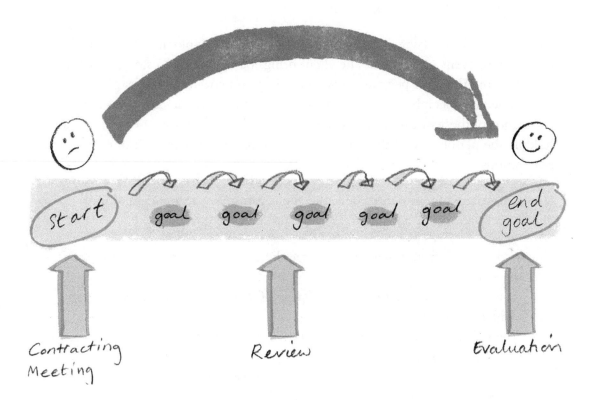

Put it into action

- Use this in contracting the assignment with both individuals and organisations.
- Share it with clients to review timing for review and evaluation.
- Hold it in mind to sustain momentum.

Making Meaning in Coaching

What this is

We value this model because it highlights the equality of the coaching relationship – it is not hierarchical or proselytising.

The coach and the client sit in the same position in the exploration of a situation, relationship, event or context. The client brings objectives and a story, which they describe from their perspective. Together, client and coach unpick, explore, discuss, decode, decipher, visualise, dream, experiment and devise. The client is the author of the work with the coach alongside focused on the same exploration, holding the perspective of the third corner to avoid joining the client in assumptions.

When this shared focus is at its best, the client gains new awareness and more choice and options for behavioural change (as does the coach).

The model comes from reflecting on what clients have said about our coaching over the years:

- *'You are an unraveller. I bring a great tangle of stuff and when I leave it's the same stuff but it's a neat ball of useful string.'*
- *'You're like the Pensieve in* Harry Potter. *I get out my thoughts and together we make sense of them.'*
- *'I come with my head full of scrunched-up newspaper. I take it out and you smooth the pages and we put them together in the right order.'*

The client is clear that the process of coaching uses their own thoughts and ideas and reframes them to make sense differently.

How we use it

- We hold this in mind to ensure that we hear more and more about the client's perspectives and together frame a different one.
- At times, we put the diagram or a representation of it on the table or the floor and physically move to another point of the triangle with the client to get a different view of what's going on.

Making Meaning in Coaching

Story through eyes of participant
& Evidence from organisation

view + explore ↗

Impact + Influence →

Awareness
Reframing
New Possibilities
Behavioural change

client
+
coach 👁👁

Context +
Organisational
values/
expectations

— — — — — — — →
view + explore

Put it into action

- Ask your clients questions about the organisation's values and expectations and how they are impacting on the story. Explore how the story might be different, if interpreted through other value sets.
- Challenge the client's assertions. *Who says? What's the evidence?*
- Reflect on other images clients have offered you that make a similar point about the coaching process. *How can you use those to explain, develop and enrich your coaching?*
- Apply this model in relation to supervision too, as described in Chapter 7. The process is similar.

The Focus of Coaching

What this is

We created the next diagram for a conference in Spain to explain the difference between coaching, mentoring for professional accreditation and supervision. Finding a visual way of making the differences clear really focused our thinking. It is related to other models in Chapter 7.

A practitioner who coaches, mentors and supervises (as we do) will use the same skill set in all these interventions. What makes the meeting one thing rather than another? We believe it is the focus of the practitioner.

There are three diagrams to show the focus when we are coaching, mentoring or supervising. Diagrams relating to mentoring and supervision come later in the book. This is the first, relating to coaching. The coach focuses on the client, who is naturally embedded in their own world.

How we use it

The world we hear about in coaching is the client's perception of their world rather than an absolute and immutable reality. We understand that their perception:
- is not everyone's perception
- is not the perception they themselves will always have
- is not the perception they would necessarily like to have
- *is* our starting point.

We explore what they tell us and also ask them to take a new view as we go.

We are alert for 'third-party coaching' – when the client tells us about someone else and the two of us together start sorting out that third person. Result? We lose focus on what the *client* can do/think/believe/contribute in the situation. So, if we notice this happening, we point out to the client that they are offering us an invitation to join them in working on an absent third party and that the only person anyone can change is themselves.

The Focus of Coaching

Put it into action

Here is our focus as coaches. The diagram above reminds us that we are working on the client's agenda, starting from their world and working with their world view.

Give this diagram to participants on coach training when they find it hard to stay with the client's agenda. Many people have been educated to give advice and solve problems, and struggle to let go of this habit. A visual reminder might help to keep them on track.

We are all sometimes asked by clients to go to a place other than coaching: giving advice, rescuing, consulting. Use this diagram to hold on to the focus and stay there when you are tempted to wear different hats, although the contract you have entered into is for coaching.

When you have multiple roles or tasks within an organisation and want to clarify your contract and offering, use this diagram in conjunction with the linked diagrams in Chapter 7 to help you.

The Coach Persona

What this is

The diagram represents the person we bring to our practice. This is the key to how we practise. As our own self-awareness, knowledge, experience and skills grow, so do the range and quality of our offer to our clients. So too does the range of issues and contexts that we are confident working with.

To be of service to others, we need to be selfish in the sense of being able to focus on and grow the self. As the centre of the self grows, so too does the span of the circle where we can operate effectively. The potential for growth is indicated in the diagram by the dotted circle. It is fed by different types of professional and personal development, indicated by the long arrows.

How we use it

This diagram reminds us about our own needs. It may help us ensure that we:
- actively reflect on our work in supervision
- seek out and take part in professional development courses
- look at what's going on inside us and how that might impact on others
- allow space for personal development
- take time to recharge ourselves
- make space to centre ourselves before client sessions.

We also use it to prompt awareness when supervising other coaches. They may be experiencing discomfort or reluctance at the growing edge of the inner circle, questioning whether they have the skills or awareness to deal with certain issues. This is natural. While it's important to have our antennae out for issues that are best taken to therapy, clunkiness or insecurity are common during the growing process, when we try out new approaches or work in unaccustomed areas.

The bigger our inner circle, the more we can do.

Put it into action

- Focus on your own practice and development. *What would push out the boundaries? What might be constricting growth? How could your professional development impact your clients?*

The Coach Persona

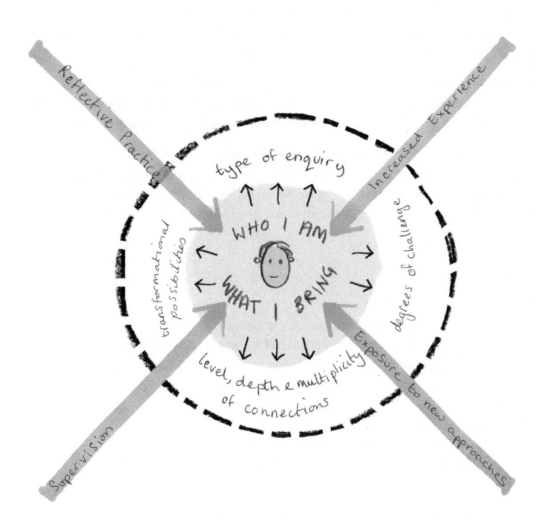

- Explain the diagram to clients. Explore the importance of personal and professional development to them. *What might push out their boundaries? How much do they want that? What else might be relevant for them?*

The Coaching Space

What this is

The enclosing arms represent the coaching space. It is safe and positive, fostering reflection and working with commitment to confidentiality. The coach has the responsibility to create and safeguard this safe space.

The two-way arrow represents the two-way process of coaching. Coach and client create a relationship together. They engage collaboratively, adjusting to each other as though in a dance. Both draw learning from their interaction.

The speech bubbles reflect the fact that most coaching is a dialogic process. Coaching is a conversation. Both coach and client speak in a context where listening may take up more space than the actual words. The diagram also indicates the thinking and feeling happening around and through the speech.

How we use it

We hold the coaching space safe by:
- holding the client's information as confidential
- taking our work to supervision and reflecting on our own process
- developing ourselves so we have more to offer our clients
- entering into clear agreements with our clients
- respecting boundaries of time, role and context
- keeping our commitments
- arriving in a state of calm and preparedness ourselves
- discontinuing the work if it ceases to benefit the client.

We respond to the client's dance by:
- regarding our client as our partner and the work as collaborative
- responding to the client's agenda, needs and learning preferences
- being alert to intuition and testing out new ways of working
- altering pace and stepping up the challenge when appropriate
- adjusting our language and approach to suit the client.

The Coaching Space

Put it into action

- Ask yourself about the boundaries that hold you and your client safe. Annotate or illustrate the diagram above to represent your practice.
- Compare the equality of the two people in the diagram to the way you think about and work with your clients. *How equal is this? How collaborative? Where is the balance in talking and listening?*
- Check what attention you pay to the unspoken.

The Baggage

What this is

The diagram highlights the hinterland in the coaching relationship. In all relationships we have, we each bring our own baggage: the total of our experiences, beliefs, values, influences, quirks, learnings and general life story. These more or less hidden aspects may be factors in, or distractors from, our choice of coach or supervisor (and indeed, partner and friends).

The meetings for client and coach to decide to work together are often called chemistry sessions – aptly named, as we are checking out how the interaction of our baggage works. And we cannot always see what goes into the mix. In fact, it is often out of our awareness.

This diagram acknowledges that baggage, or hinterland, exists for all of us and is at work in the relational space at all stages of the coaching. It has a huge and often unacknowledged influence on how we act and the way our relationships with others develop. It shapes our coaching and how we interact with clients whether we like it or not.

How we use it

We take our coaching practice to supervision to develop our awareness of what's in our baggage and how it is impacting on the way we show up for our clients and interact with them.

We spend time reflecting on what we have learnt about the patterns of behaviour and thought that we have discovered.

We might use this diagram to help our clients reflect on what baggage they might be carrying and what they might like to let go of, once it's in their awareness. Baggage is often heavy, and letting go of it can create new energy and release people to see things with fresh eyes.

The Baggage

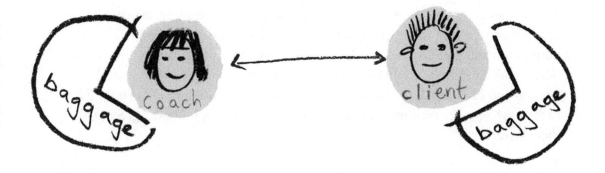

Put it into action

- Remind yourself of the complex influences in relationships.
- Ask clients to reflect on what is at play in their relationships.
- Normalise the complexity – explain that relationships are one of the most common issues brought to coaching.
- Explore the hidden hinterlands without judgement.

Levels of the Coaching Contract

What this is

This diagram represents all the levels and types of contracting that are present in coaching assignments within organisations.

The top-level 'organisational contract' is the status and definition of coaching adopted as policy by the organisation. It includes a definition of coaching, the purpose for the organisation, who is eligible, how much coaching is allowed, in what conditions, how it will be evaluated, how return on investment will be assessed and how much the organisation will invest in coaching in both time and money. Many organisations set out to introduce coaching without agreeing all these features.

The three-way contract is the agreement between the coachee, their line manager or sponsor and the coach, aligning the aims of the organisation for the coaching intervention with the aims of the individual client for their own coaching. It also covers how the coaching will be evaluated and what feedback will be given within the context of a truly confidential relationship between coach and client.

On the left is the continuing brief of the organisation, to monitor and support progress. On the right, we note that a psychological contract always exists: it's the unspoken mutual expectations of inputs and outcomes. The coach may not be fully aware of organisational psychological contracts.

How we use it

We use this model to explore with trainee coaches and organisations:
- how coaching is going to be used in a particular context
- what to consider when establishing coaching as an organisational tool or entitlement
- what to agree at each level of the contract.

Put it into action

Use this diagram to help you create a checklist of things to consider and agree with corporate clients and sponsors as you set up the coaching relationship.

Levels of the Coaching Contract

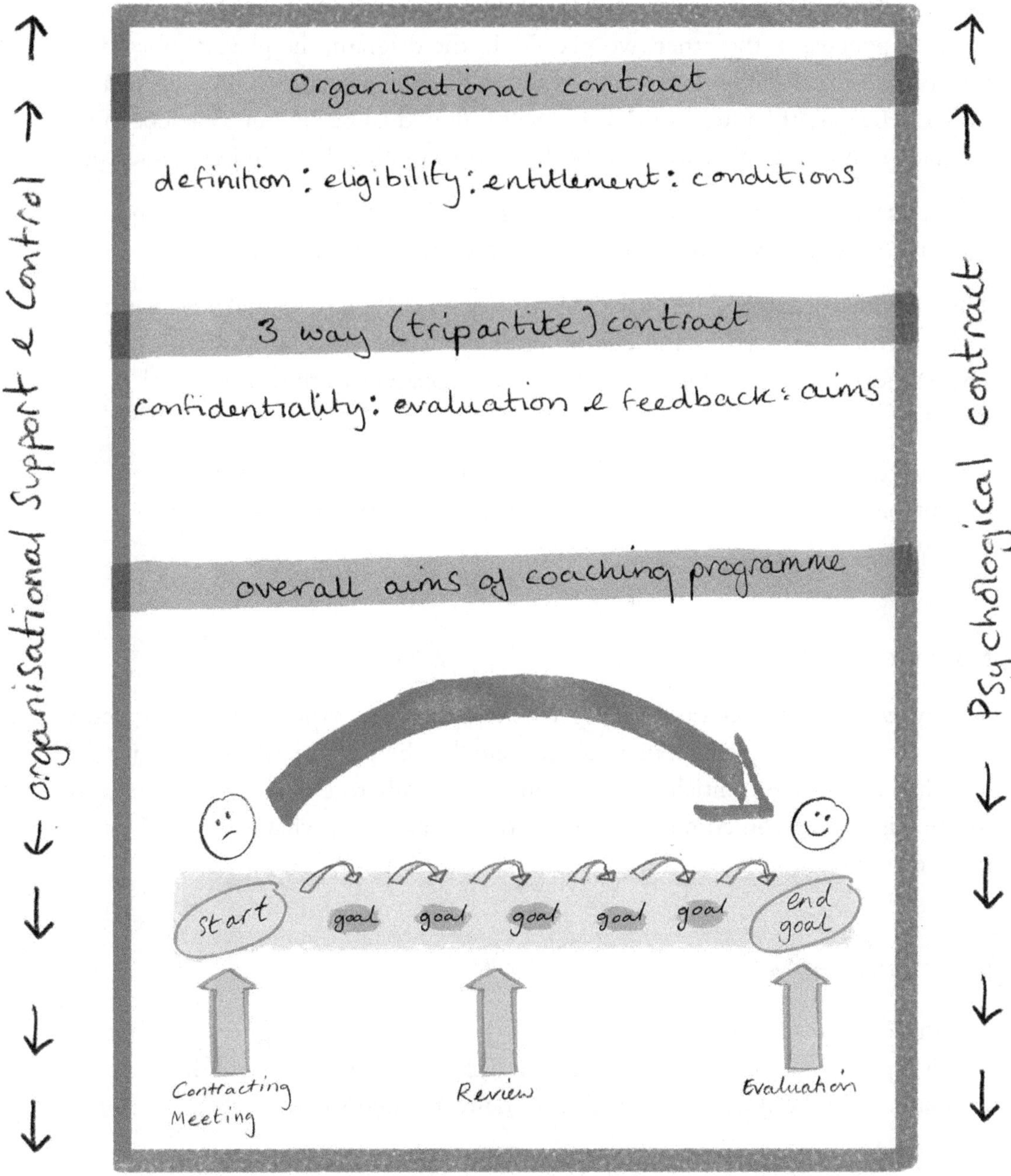

The Tripartite Meeting: Agendas and Drivers

What this is

A corporate or executive coaching assignment usually starts with a tripartite meeting. Each party, including the coach, has an agenda. The coach also aims to align the agendas of the other two people. In the diagram, the players' objectives for the meeting sit behind each one of them, like the baggage we described earlier. They are the often-unseen drivers of individual behaviour. The coach has complex contractual obligations to both the organisational and individual client.

The sponsor's overarching objective is to gain value for the organisation and to support the employee to develop in order to deliver corporate aims.

The individual coachee seeks personal development, organisational advancement and sometimes also has desired outcomes that are apparently at odds with the organisational aims. They may also have some apparently entirely personal objectives.

The coach seeks to agree an explicit agenda for the coaching with clear, measurable outcomes, protected confidentiality and a transparent feedback process.

How we use it

We always seek a three-way meeting when engaged in corporate coaching and we are often asked to explain (sometimes repeatedly) the purpose of the meeting. We have had the coachee initially express reluctance, only to embrace the value of the meeting and hear, sometimes for the first time apparently, what the organisation requires.

Put it into action

Use this diagram to explain the benefits of the tripartite meeting to your clients. It will support you all to see and understand the different drivers for different stakeholders in the intervention and so to deliver added value.

The Tripartite Meeting

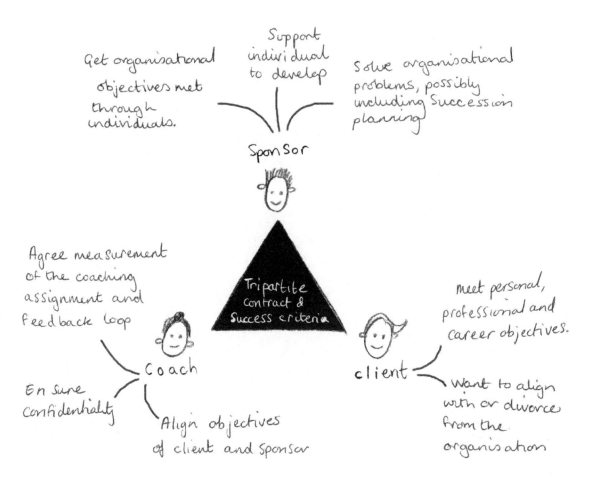

Get organisational objectives met through individuals.

Support individual to develop

Solve organisational problems, possibly including Succession planning

Sponsor

Agree measurement of the coaching assignment and feedback loop

Ensure confidentiality

Coach

Align objectives of client and Sponsor

Tripartite contract & Success criteria

meet personal, professional and career objectives.

client

Want to align with or divorce from the organisation

Chapter 3

Relationships and Communication

Relationships and Communication

We often meet managers and leaders who are concerned about relationships and communication. How simple it would be if management was just about logistics, problem-solving, design, rational thinking – and not complex people.

Managers are successful when they working effectively with others. Leaders work with teams to reach shared, articulated goals. Both must build productive relationships, consider the part others play (or choose not to play), and communicate openly, clearly and confidently in different situations.

Most businesses and organisations say their people are their greatest asset: many fewer actually take time out for reflection or consider people first when they design projects, disseminate ideas, order changes, set new requirements and 'develop' the business. Indeed, we recently heard one CEO say there was no time for reflection in his organisation at the moment because they were engaged in a project of cultural change.

Relationships and communication are of key importance when we grapple with 'wicked issues' – those uncertainties, complex issues, unknowables and unguessables of our many-layered global society – that beset many of today's organisations.

Horst W. J. Rittel and Melvin M. Webber, professors of design and urban planning at the University of California at Berkeley, originally described 'wicked issues' in a 1973 article in *Policy Sciences* magazine. Other strategists and analytical thinkers have elaborated on the concept since then.

Wicked problems have innumerable causes, are tough to describe and don't have a 'right' answer. In other words, we don't know much about them. One of the few things we do know is that we cannot solve them on our own. Understanding others, interacting and communicating well with them lie at the heart of finding possible solutions. Clear and strong cooperative relationships and effective communication are fundamental for leaders to succeed in our increasingly interconnected and complex world.

This chapter looks at what goes on when we communicate and how we build and experience relationships. When we look at our work connections and familiar messages through the framework of a diagram or model, we are often able to take the heat out of relationships, acknowledge the needs of both the organisation and the individual, and move forward. Externalisation, frameworks and reflection help us to understand the personal styles and concerns that impact on what may, in theory, seem to be an impersonal organisation, so that we can create more effective relationships and modes of communication.

Seeing a representation of a situation or relationship gives our clients scope for thinking differently about how things are and how they might be. We invite you to use the diagrams here to help your clients gain new perspectives. The models are not cast in stone. Make them your own and follow the trail the client lays.

We include diagrams that relate to:
- the process of communication
- what influences the way we communicate with each other
- the impact of the unconscious on our interactions
- increasing our ability to manage ourselves
- narrowing the gap when we have conflicting ways forward
- unproductive roles we get caught up in
- how to move to more productive roles in our interactions.

Communication Model

What this is

Communication theory developed out of codebreaking in the Second World War. Since then, people have adapted a diagram created by Claude Elwood Shannon and Warren Weaver in 1949 for use in telecommunications, and used it as a psychological (or media-psychological) model. The model shows how our experiences and understanding, which we might call mental and emotional baggage, and psychologists might term schemata, both filter and interrupt our communication with others.

As an illustration, we (Sarah and Jenny) can only speak as educated European women. We can't turn off our education, race or cultural background as a default filter, though we may learn not to be totally limited by it. The influence of our world view leaks into all our communication. Our responses are influenced by, and contain elements of, all that we are. This happens whether we are writing, texting, speaking, dancing; similarly, everyone we communicate with experiences and decodes the world in their unique way.

The middle section of our diagram depicts the interference with the intended message from both the medium chosen for communication and from external and internal noise: mismatches of language, our own thoughts and feelings, interruptions, etc. The chances of the thought that started in my head arriving whole and identical in yours are negligible!

How we use it

We use this diagram to help people explore how their message may be received by others, particularly when we hear comments such as, '*Everyone knows that . . .*', '*Why doesn't he realise that. . .*' and '*It's obvious*', which assume that we all process the world the same. We:
*   talk through the fact that we each have our own filters
*   discuss how others may see or hear what we say
*   ask how they might uncover what's going on
*   ask what they'd like to do differently as a result of this discussion.

Communication Model

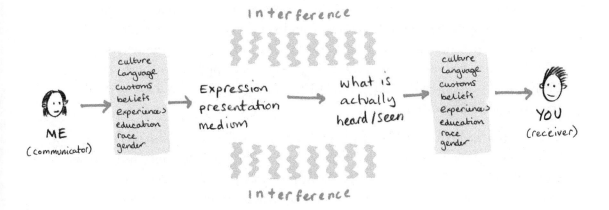

Put it into action

Reflect on this model when you or the people you are working with:
- can't understand why your message isn't getting across
- aren't sure what weight to give to comments on 360° feedbacks
- notice repeated patterns of behaviour
- want to decode other people's actions
- are thinking about a new recruit's possible expectations
- are building cross-cultural understanding in the organisation.

You could:
- get individuals to identify what might be in their world-view box
- invite others to describe what is in their world-view box
- consider the differences
- ask how we would receive different messages and what we might say differently if we started from a different perspective
- check back what people have heard and might want to hear
- experiment with rephrasing your messages. Note the impact to help you remember and plan how to communicate next time.

Communication Pie

What this is

This pie chart represents the relative impact of body language, tone of voice and words on how a listener receives a spoken message. The percentages are not absolute. They are based on a small-scale and very specific study by Albert Mehrabian, an American professor of psychology, into the communication of feelings and attitudes. However, some people have applied his equation *Total Liking = 7% Verbal Liking + 38% Vocal Liking + 55% Facial Liking* to all types of communication.

So there is a widespread belief that 55 per cent of our message comes across in our body language, 38 per cent in our tone of voice and just 7 per cent in the actual words we choose. These percentages have probably gained currency because they resonate with our experience. We are uneasy when someone's non-verbal messages contradict their verbal ones.

If someone tells us they appreciate our work, but mutter under their breath and fail to smile or look at us in the eye, we don't believe them. We notice a lack of congruence between the person's words, tone of voice and body language and are likely to believe the message from the non-verbal clues, not the words. This is difficult for leaders who are not tuned into their own body language, as research tells us that what people most want from them is honesty.

How we use it

We explore different communication channels with people who want to communicate more effectively with others. We:
- explain that words, body language and tone of voice must all carry the same message for communication to be unambiguous
- use the slices of the pie like different lenses to separate what people say from how they say it, and from what others see as they speak
- ask about situations when they have felt someone was not open
- experiment with different ways of saying similar phrases or words.

Communication Pie

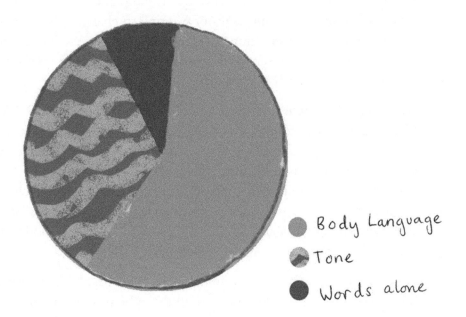

Put it into action

- Ask your clients what happens when they can't fully subscribe to the company message they have to give to other people.
- Find out where in the body they feel this and how it impacts on their tone of voice or speed of speaking.
- Ask what is different about tone, pace and body language when they wholeheartedly believe the message they have to give.
- Consider together how this could impact on what other people see or hear and what different responses this could lead to.
- Ask what might need to change.
- Practise different ways of speaking and behaving in a safe space.
- Observe, give feedback, and reflect together on movement, gesture and tone.

Internal Responses: Changing Ourselves or Others?

What this is

Our picture illustrates the impact of our feelings and internal judgements on others. Most of us have moments of wanting to change other people's behaviour. We may think that instructing, creating rules and implementing sanctions or rewards will work. It rarely does! However, changing our own internal response can be a powerful lever for change.

As we have seen, what we think and feel about others translates itself into our body language, our tone of voice and our choice of words. All these give out messages to the people we are talking to, who pick up these clues and respond to them emotionally. This in turn influences how much of our verbal message they really hear. As a result, their tone of voice, body language and choice of words change. This is what we observe – their message to us. We respond emotionally. Our thoughts and judgements shift. Our tone of voice and body language alter. And so the communication cycle continues.

When we feel confident and calm, all sorts of verbal and non-verbal clues make the outcome of a conversation more likely to be positive. Conversely, when we feel doubtful, suspicious and judgemental, we transmit a different message and the outcome is likely to be unproductive or worse.

How we use it

We explain the diagram to clients and use it to help people reflect on:
- what they can/cannot control
- what is going on for them when they meet 'difficult' colleagues
- how this influences what others see and hear
- how to shift their own internal messages.

Internal Responses

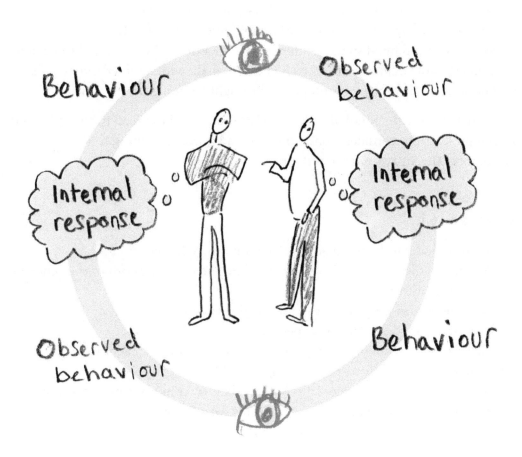

Put it into action

You may find that some people respond to this model as though the theory is all very well but reality is different. So that you can really experience its power and speak with conviction, we suggest you:

- use it yourself to reflect on a relationship you find challenging
- consider how else you might perceive the person in question (e.g. changing from *defensive* to *shy or nervous*)
- during the meeting, visualise a positive outcome, with you both leaving the room relaxed and smiling – hold this image in mind
- note what happens and experiment again.

Interactional Triangle

What this is

We drew this during a group supervision, as one of us described a three-way working relationship that was not working because of the agendas, drivers, preoccupations and blind spots of other people in a team. As we started to explore what these factors might be, we sketched this triangle with a hinterland behind each person and then began to fill out what might be going on for them.

Each circle represents an individual in a relationship, and the shadow circle behind them represents the considerations, concerns and needs they bring to the interaction. The arrows represent the relational flow.

How we use it

We use this model to help someone to see other people's positions:
- We invite the client to discuss, or write in, the considerations of the other players in a situation.
- We might map this out on the floor and invite them to stand in the shoes (or at least the space) of the other people.
- We might place empty chairs around a table and ask the client to sit in different people's chairs in turn, to gain a different perspective.
- We also use it to help people to look at their own motivators, especially when they are making 'It's not me. It's the others!' noises.

Put it into action

- Use this diagram to explore motivation, drivers and stories, either in writing or in discussion.
- Invite someone to create a similar diagram or a tactile imago using objects to illuminate what's going on in a multi-level interaction between three or more players. We did this effectively with a box of teabags in a recent supervision group. Use whatever is to hand!

Interactional Triangle

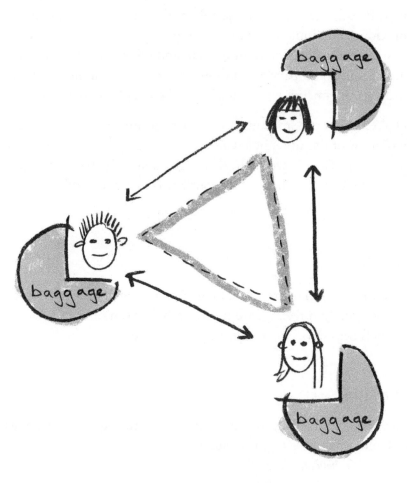

Iceberg

What this is

You may remember this image from the cover of the book! Many people, starting with Sigmund Freud, have used the metaphor of an iceberg to illustrate the fact that our conscious and visible behaviour is only a small part of who we actually are. What we see is the product of an unseen, and often unconscious, mass of values, beliefs, feelings and patterns of thought. The large submerged mass of the iceberg represents the unconscious, which may be deeply hidden from our view.

Freud also talked about the 'preconscious' – part of our memory that we are not very aware of most of the time, but which we can easily access when we need it. It's just below the surface. If we wish to change habits of behaviour, working with the values and beliefs that lie beneath the surface is likely to produce the most powerful and long-lasting results.

How we use it

We have used this diagram most in training. It is a graphic introduction to the idea of how thoughts and feelings are linked to behaviour, and of how embedded values and beliefs impact on the results people achieve.

Put it into action

Hold this image in mind when working with clients to acquire new habits and behaviours. Useful questions might include:
*   *What's going on beneath the surface?*
*   *What's the story underpinning this?*
*   *What are the rules here?*
*   *How does this connect with your values?*
*   *How does this fit with your beliefs?*
*   *What would you have to believe if you were to behave differently?*

Iceberg

Johari Window

What this is

The Johari Window, created originally by Joseph Luft and Harrington Ingham, helps us to see what we reveal to the world, what we keep hidden from others and what we don't (yet) know about ourselves. The diagram here draws on the work of Bruce Peltier. It shows the way the public area of knowledge spreads through feedback and disclosure to impact on personal and professional growth:

- Those aspects of ourselves that are known both to us and people we interact with are shown in the top left quadrant of the diagram. This area is fluid. It grows as we receive feedback from others and disclose more of ourselves to those around us.
- Top right are the aspects that are not known to us and to which we are blind. Think 360° feedback, which can be a surprise to us!
- On the bottom left is the area of our secrets – things we know about ourselves but are unwilling or unable to present to the world.
- Finally, the bottom right is the home of the unconscious, which is not known either to us or to others.

Many people know of the Johari Window and find it useful in relationship work, especially for introducing feedback. Our diagram helps to illustrate the potential to extend the public area through feedback, coaching, learning and development, and other supportive interventions.

How we use it

With a group, we:
- ask how willing each person is to receive feedback and expand their public area (how open they would like colleagues to be!)
- create guidelines together to keep the interactions manageable
- ensure that everyone sticks to agreed behaviour.

In workshops and team development work, we:
- agree together about how we will deliver and receive feedback
- use the diagram to help the participants consider their intentions when they tell others how they experience them.

Personal and Professional Growth

Put it into action

Support your client to:
- consider what they know about themselves (the left-hand side)
- think about their responses to feedback and how they use it
- consider what they might like to change about their self-knowledge and how teams or colleagues could help
- use the diagram to help create space for feedback and mutual understanding in the team.

Emotional Intelligence Cone

What this is

This diagram is a way into understanding emotional intelligence, a concept that Daniel Goleman has written much about. We work best with others when we understand and manage our own emotional responses first. In this model, all the movement starts from awareness of self. When we know how we process things and respond, we can manage ourselves better. We also notice the behaviour of others and pause before we react, rather than responding impulsively without considering the consequences for everyone. This model helps us create space, respond as we would wish and develop respect for other people who behave differently from us. That bit of space for understanding may save us from the knee-jerk reactions that damage relationships.

How we use it

This is another great model to use as part of team building. We:
- describe it
- use it to agree codes of behaviour and communication processes
- ask teams to consider how they work together and respond to each other and whether this is how they really want to interact
- encourage more conscious choice in interactions and relationships.

Put it into action

We all move through a variety of emotions during a day – some brief and some more sustained, some strong and some low level. It can be a revelation to notice these as we experience them rather than just going with the emotional flow. Use the steps below for yourself or with clients:
- Relate this diagram to your own thoughts in the day to day: focus on your own passing emotions and responses for a while.
- Analyse what is going on. '*I notice I am angry: Jane has just left the room and I feel furious. I was very brusque with her.*'
- Think a bit more deeply. Was the anger triggered by an email before Jane came in, a word she used that reminded you of something else, or something connected with Jane that you did not address assertively, but responded to in a coded way by being brusque?

Emotional Intelligence Cone

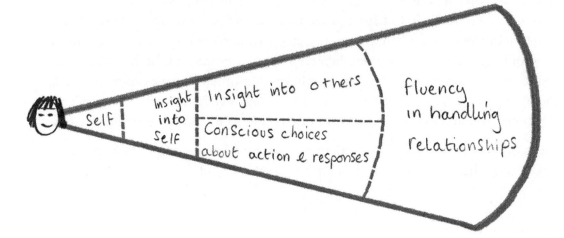

Encourage clients having a difficult relationship with someone to:

- think about themselves first
- share the diagram with the other person, and discuss what's going on and potential miscommunications or mismatches of behaviour
- remember that it takes time, thought and sensitivity to develop (and help others develop) emotionally intelligent behaviour.

Drama Triangle

What this is

Developed by Karpman (1968), the Drama Triangle describes three characteristic positions that people may take up in interactions with others. Each sees us replaying ineffective patterns of thoughts and behaviour. At different times, with different people, in different contexts, we may take up different positions. However, we are likely to have a propensity for one position over others. When we take our position, we may be responding to a hook from someone else and we in turn hook others, so that they then take up their positions relative to us. As we do so, we often respond to triggers that have their origins in past experience and lie outside our conscious awareness. It's rather like a vicious dance into which we lock ourselves and each other. We are often blind to the positions we have taken.

Each of these positions is characterised by patterns of thought, speech, behaviour and feeling that can be observed, surfaced and challenged.

How we use it

The work of Napper and Newton (2000) has influenced our thinking on both the Drama Triangle and its positive partner, the Winners' Triangle, which follows. We have found that certain clients (for instance, people working in the caring professions in particular) may risk burnout because they are trapped in the Rescuer role. We find that explaining the model to clients, with or without the elaborated diagrams on the following pages, can help them to gain new awareness of how they might be sabotaging themselves. With awareness comes the potential for change and for moving to the corresponding position on the Winners' Triangle.

Put it into action

This model is all the more powerful when you have had the uncomfortable personal revelation about your own potential to play out a role in the Drama Triangle. Ask yourself and others:

- *Where and when might you be caught in the triangle yourself?*

Drama Triangle

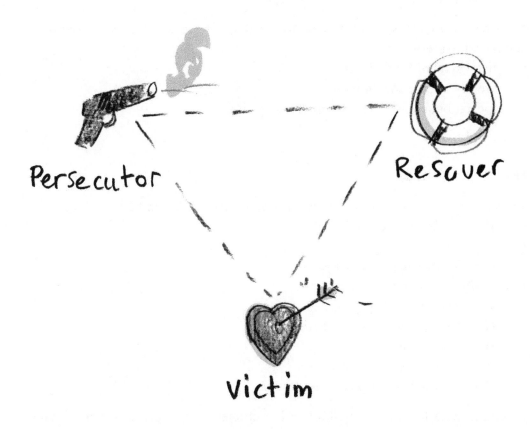

Persecutor

Resover

Victim

Drama Triangle

What the next three diagrams are

The following three pages expand on what might be going on, as individuals play out the Rescuer, Victim or Persecutor roles.

We have used visual symbols to help to separate out types of feelings, thoughts and speech patterns:

- heart symbol for feelings
- woolly bubble for thoughts
- speech bubble for what we might be saying.

How we use this

We show a sheet focused on a relevant position to a client and ask:

- *What might you recognise?*
- *What's going on for you?*
- *How do others respond when you say that?*
- *Which position might they be in?*
- *What might be hooking you?*
- *How might you be hooking others?*
- *What's the impact for you?*
- *What's the impact for others?*
- *Where, when and with whom does this happen?*

Listening and following the trail might be sufficient for insight and change. The client might also take one or all of these diagrams away for reflection.

Put it into action

- Reflect on your own tendencies.
- Take time to understand each position.
- Ask yourself questions about what's going on for you.
- Be kind to yourself – we all have a propensity to be trapped in this dance. That's where the 'drama' comes in!
- Take the benefit of your understanding to your work with others.

What might be going on for the Rescuer . . .

capable
overburdened
righteous

It's ok
I feel for you
I'll do that for you
You can have more time
Don't worry about me

I need to
help

I serve
others

I'm responsible
for it all

I'm carrying
everyone

They can't
manage

I have to work
so hard

Persecutor

Victim

Rescuer

What might be going on for the Persecutor . . .

What may be going on for the Victim . . .

Persecutor   Rescuer

Victim

It's all too much for me

I can't think what to do

Nothing will help

There's no choice

Why does this always happen to me?

I've got so much going on for me, you can't expect me to . . .
You're so good at it
I never got that help when I was a child

Fearful
Singled out
Self pitying

He's always picking on me.
There's not enough time to do it.
The System just doesn't allow it

Winners' Triangle

What this is

How wonderful that there is an antidote to the Drama Triangle! Developed by Choy (1990), it offers us a way out of our entrenched positions so that we can be lighter in ourselves and develop more productive relationships with others. Key elements of the escape route are described by Napper and Newton (2000), and help us to move to positions in which we each accept the other as 'OK'.

To move out of the Victim role, we voice what's going on for us, owning and taking responsibility for our feelings, thoughts, reactions and vulnerability.

To move out of the Persecutor role, we give positive strokes to others, explicitly recognising their value and skills; accept that most people do the best they can do, given the experience and knowledge they have to date; and actively use mistakes and unexpected outcomes to learn and develop.

To move out of the Rescuer role, we develop awareness of our own role and the roles others fill, of our responsibilities and what others are responsible for. We agree these boundaries proactively and commit to staying within them, delivering what we have promised and no more or less than asked.

How we use it

- We explain to clients the different positions that players in a situation might be holding and ask what this might mean for them.
- We support clients as they unpick and rebuild deep-seated beliefs or views of the world that are influencing the roles they play.
- We help shift beliefs so people can say something positive to someone else with sincerity. A positive stroke is powerful when belief and body language are congruent with the words offered – the message is more likely to be heard and internalised.
- We help people give voice to what is going on for them in the moment.

Winners' Triangle

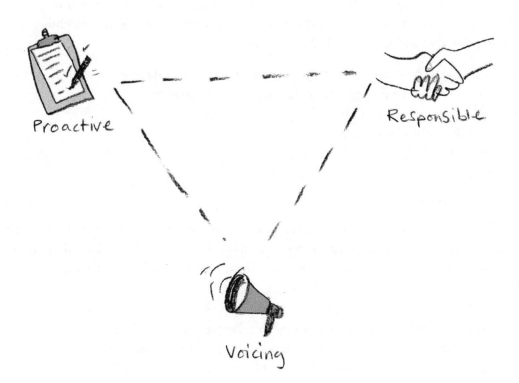

Proactive

Responsible

Voicing

Put it into action

When someone has understood where they sit on the Drama Triangle, use this model to help them move into a more positive position. Give them time to explore and rehearse the choices they have.

The Drama Triangle shows them the bottomless pit. The Winners' Triangle offers them a ladder out.

Winners' Triangle

What the next three diagrams are

The next three pages expand on the shifts in feeling, thought and speech that individuals need to move into winning positions, through taking responsibility, being proactive and voicing what's going on.

We have used the same visual symbols as in the Drama Triangle above to help to separate out types of feelings, thoughts and speech patterns:
- heart symbol for feelings
- woolly bubble for thoughts
- speech bubble for what we might be saying.

How we use it

Having identified which role someone has a propensity for, or which role they are playing out in a particular relationship, we might explain the behaviour that could help them move to the corresponding winners' position. We would ask questions that related to that particular position, for example:
- *What is your role here? And your colleague's role?*
- *What are your responsibilities? And your colleague's responsibilities?*
- *What might you need to think in order to keep to your own role?*
- *What do you need to think about your colleague for this to happen?*
- *If you thought that, what might you say? What else?*
- *And how would you feel as a result of this?*
- *What support do you need to follow this through?*

Put it into action

To help you surface patterns and offer the possibility of change both to yourself and your clients:
- practise non-judgemental curiosity and acceptance
- recognise the person
- normalise the experience, explaining that anyone can get hooked
- offer both support and challenge in reframing thoughts and beliefs.

Being Responsible might include . . .

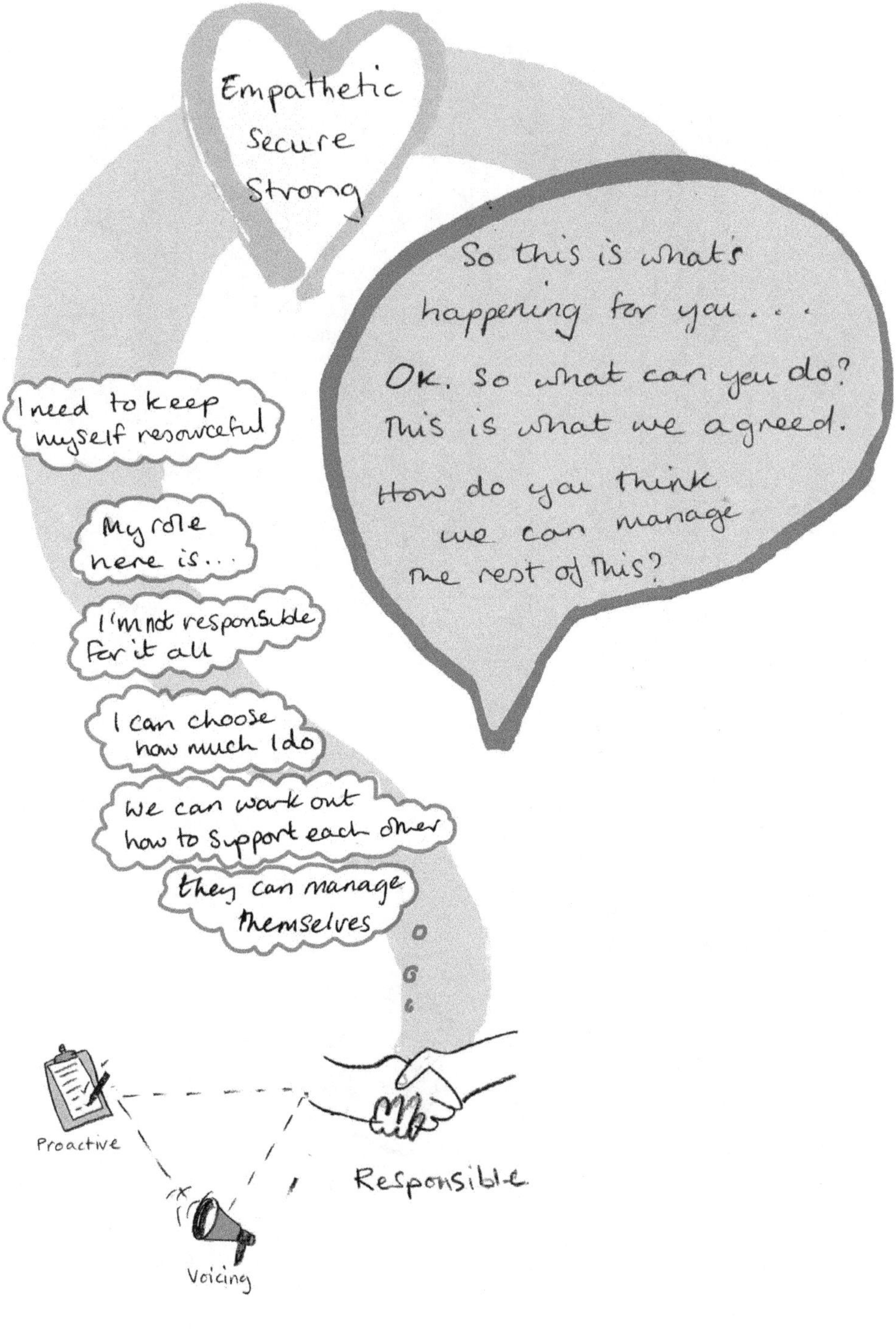

Being Proactive might include . . .

Collaborative
Encouraged
Light

What's the learning?
How can we use it?
I value your opinion.

When is it manageable?
What role do we each play?
What else can we all agree?

We could make some adjustments to timing

He does well with support

Looking at what didn't go so well last time will help us do better

We can find a way together

She's got lots of skills

We all make mistakes

Proactive

Responsible

Voicing

Voicing might include . . .

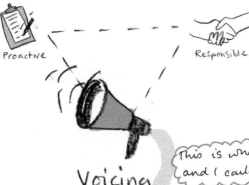

Proactive

Responsible

Voicing

This is what I feel – and I could just be over reacting

I could try something new and see if it works

Maybe I don't need to do it all

Maybe I don't need to do it so well

It's ok to ask for help with my decisions

I can say NO if I want to

This is how I feel about it
I'd like to find a way to organise things differently
If it doesn't work, I'll try something else
It would help me to talk this through

When this happens, I react by thinking...
I'd like to check this out...
I need more time to work out some alternatives

Experimental
Self-accepting
Interested

Chapter 4

Learning and Personal Growth

Learning and Personal Growth

All the ideas and models in this book are, in one sense, about learning and personal growth. We work in that space ourselves, and work with other Learning and Development professionals and coaches to help them create great learning experiences for individuals, teams and groups.

The idea of a learning economy is compelling, and where years ago many leaders would have said that the company is 'as good as its people', they would now say that an organisation is as good as its people's ability to learn, develop, innovate and adapt. The speed of communication, technical development, international interchange and innovation mean that organisations compete to find the best ways of creating learning environments.

We have recently worked with the leaders of an organisation that was in the forefront of renewable energy with a groundbreaking invention twenty years ago: the whole aim of the project was to find and embed ways of keeping the company and its people innovative and agile in the context of organisational growth, which requires standardisation and processes. This is a common dilemma: the tension between the need for consistency and regulation within an organisation or industry, and the need for free thinking and creative responses from employees. In effect, we are simultaneously asking people to play by the rules and to think outside the box.

Keeping learning fresh and dynamic in twenty-first-century businesses is vital.

We know that people learn better (or at least differently) when using diagrams and drawings. There is a huge advantage in group work when we use a model because it shorthands the joint experience and allows us to convey complex concepts with a mere 'that' or 'in the xxx model'.

Developments in neuroscience show us that by using a diagram, we are liberating more of the brain to make other connections and to be creative. It is also clear that use of a model as well as words allows learning to be accessed through a range of approaches, so that it becomes more accessible.

So in this chapter, we explore both how we learn and how we can use models to support that learning further.

Some of the models in this chapter are familiar to established professionals; some are original creations. We bring new insights to extend understanding for individuals and groups.

There are models for:
• the learning cycle
• interpreting events differently
• reframing negative interpretations and changing behaviour
• stages in learning and competence: comfort, stretch, panic
• understanding the context for change
• recording strengths.

The Learning Cycle

What this is

The learning cycle is a good place to start as it describes how we work with our clients. They process experience to understand it, learn from it and make choices about how to go forward and how to change their behaviour (or not!). So, of course, do we.

There are several versions of the learning cycle, with varying numbers of stages. Their essence is summed up by the three words Plan–Do–Review.

Different people have preferences for lingering in a stage they feel comfortable with, to the neglect of other stages. However, to learn effectively and bring the impact of the learning into the workplace, all the stages are essential.

We offer you first our own version of this cycle and then match it roughly against two other well-known models.

How we use it

We might ask our clients:
- *Where are you most at ease?*
- *What stages of the cycle are you tempted to avoid?*
- *Where are other people in the team most at ease?*
- *What do their different preferences contribute?*

Put it into action

Before you use this with clients, consider:
- *Where are you most comfortable yourself?*
- *What are the implications for working with different clients?*
- *What might you be avoiding in your coaching business?*

The Learning Cycle

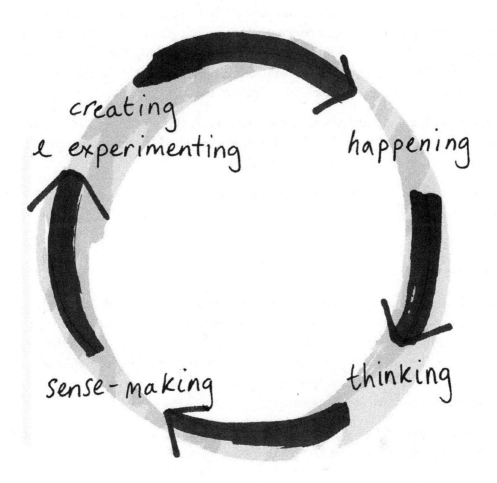

Experiential Learning Cycle

What this is

The best-known work in this area is by David Kolb, who published his 'learning styles model' in 1984. He talks about four different stages: concrete experience, reflective observation, abstract conceptualisation and active experimentation. Peter Honey and Alan Mumford built on Kolb's work to develop their learning styles theory, labelling people who have a preference for learning in the four different stages as activists, reflectors, theorists or pragmatists.

These models were widely used in education in the UK from the 1980s, though there is now debate about their benefits to teaching and learning, and indeed whether there is any evidence of their validity.

We have matched Kolb's and Honey and Mumford's terminology to our own rather simpler model opposite.

How we use it

Our clients may use some of the terms in these models to describe themselves, because they have used a diagnostic on learning style, which has framed their understanding of themselves and their preferences. Being familiar with the concepts and language ourselves helps us to enter into our clients' frame of reference and explore their understanding of themselves, their teams and their organisational context more effectively.

The models also help us and our clients understand the range of thinking brought to the same task by people with different preferences.

Put it into action

Ask your clients:
- *What would help you at uncomfortable stages in the learning cycle?*
- *How might you adjust to work with people who think differently?*

Experiential Learning Cycle

creating
+ experimenting
active experimentation: doing
planning the next steps:
pragmatist

happening
concrete experience: feeling
having an experience:
activist

thinking
reflective observation: watching
reviewing the experience:
reflector

Sense-making
abstract conceptualisation: thinking
concluding the experience:
theorist

Here we have
OUR wording
David Kolb's categorisation
Honey & Mumford's
categorisation

Cycles in Psychological Models

What this is

Most psychological traditions offer a cycle to explain how we experience and process the world: how we experience stimuli and make sense of them for ourselves. These cycles may also be used to identify how we have come to hold certain beliefs about the world or create habitual responses, some of which are not useful for us as we develop and enter new situations.

Some of these cycles have four steps and some three; some include the initial experience and some only our responses to it.

Here's our own fusion, with six steps, based on our reading of several psychological traditions. We offer it not as a process to use, but more as a way of considering how we each remake our understanding of the world based on our own experiences. We often hear that perception is reality; perhaps we should say *our processing makes our reality*.

How we use it

Here are some beliefs that clients have shared with us:
- *'You can't turn down work.'*
- *'Something will turn up.'*
- *'You're not meant to enjoy your job.'*

Apart from asking, *'Who says?'* we look at this process cycle with a client and unpick the chain of their responses, thoughts and feelings in relation to an experience, and explore how these both connect to action and reinforce their initial perception.

Put it into action

Explore the cycle with the client. Changing perception/response at one stage will impact the outcomes. Ask clients, *'What triggered that response?'*, *'Where does that belief come from?'*, *'What happens if you reframe it?'*, and *'And what happens next?'*

Cycles in Psychological Models

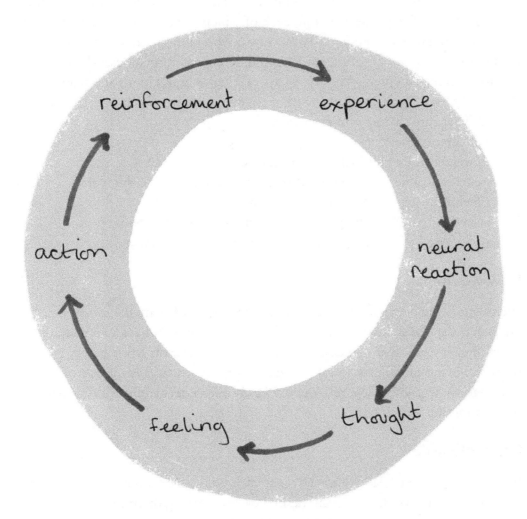

Cycle of Negative/Positive/Neutral Self-Talk

What this is

Here, we have three diagrams to show how the cycle above can play out in three different ways – negative, positive and neutral. The same trigger can lead to three different chains of response/reaction, each of which is likely to self-perpetuate. All our examples start with the same event, a boss who talks sparingly. Different reactions on the part of the listener lead to different interpretations, which in turn lead to different outcomes. We are always making interpretations and telling ourselves stories. The aim of this work is to give us more choice over the stories we tell. There are six stages in each cycle:

1   a concrete experience
2   an immediate subliminal reaction (inevitably subjective)
3   a conscious interpretation, reflecting a subjective view of the world
4   a feeling arising from the interpretation
5   behaviour based on the interpretation and emotional response to it
6   a reinforced thought, leading to a repetition of the behaviour.

How we use it

We might be proactive about starting the drawing, or offering the model. However, the client does the analysis of their thinking or behavioural patterns. Then they explore their choices. We may offer feedback on what we have observed, being careful not to call our guesswork the truth! The degree of challenge we engage in depends, of course, on our understanding of the client and our relationship with them.

Put it into action

Invite the client to consider alternatives at each point. Our three diagrams demonstrate some of these. Create desired cycles, inviting them to explore other responses and potential new outcomes.
You could ask:

*   *What might someone else think here?*
*   *How else might you see this?*
*   *What action would you ideally like to take?*
*   *What would you have to believe to be able to do that?*
*   *How could you behave in order to get that sort of reaction?*

Negative Cycle

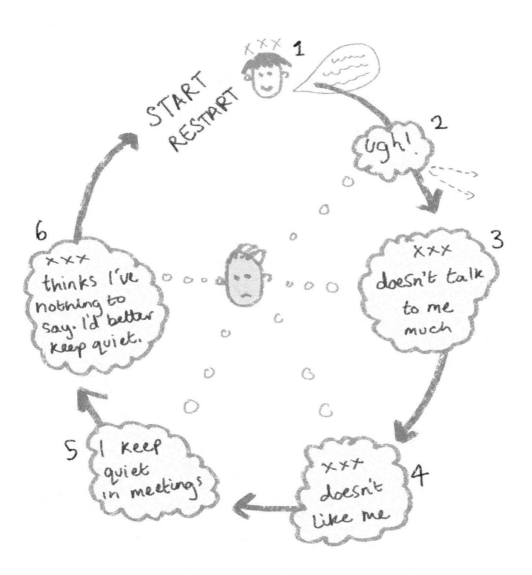

Positive Cycle

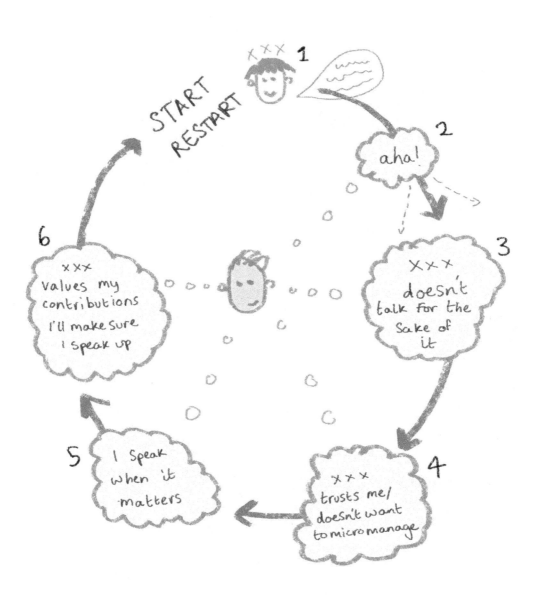

Neutral Cognitive Cycle

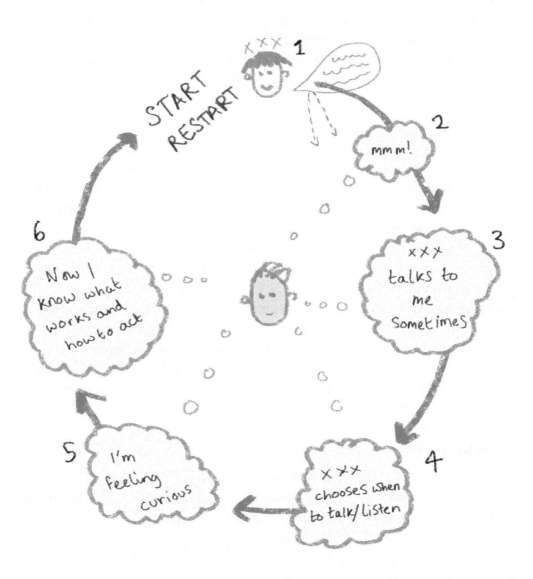

Vicious Circles and Virtuous Spirals

What this is

People often use the term 'a vicious circle' to describe a process that incrementally drains their energy and negates their positive intentions. They talk more rarely about virtuous spirals! Both are processes where once we are caught up, there is an ongoing impetus leading us further in the same direction, maybe without our noticing initially what is happening.

How we use it

One client was responsible for two teams, A and B. With team A, she was full of energy and able to give them clear direction. They outperformed their targets. With team B, she appeared to be a totally different person. She was worried about asking them to do simple tasks and unclear about the boundaries of her authority. She felt tearful at the mere thought of a team meeting. Team B had very poor performance. We used sketches of a virtuous spiral and a vicious circle to analyse what set each process in action and how this led to a pattern of effective or ineffective thinking and behaviour. With this awareness, the client was able to identify ways of kicking back against negative triggers and of setting in motion a more productive process. Working with her body initially, she gained the confidence to give team B a clear idea of her vision for them and their role in achieving it. Their performance and absence record improved over time.

Put it into action

If you pick up on a feeling that a client is being dragged down progressively, ask them where they are now in relation to either spiral and what would be different if the spiral was going the other way. Consider these questions:
- *Where do you see yourself at the moment?*
- *What's the energy driving this movement?*
- *What would you like to be different?*
- *How could you start to turn the process round?*

Vicious Circles/Virtuous Spirals

Stars and Clouds

What this is

This is a simple visual tool for using with individuals or groups to get a more balanced picture of what's going on, clarify what's going well and chunk down difficulties into discrete areas or projects. The stars represent good things on the horizon or achievements and successes to build on. The clouds represent threats and worries on the horizon or current challenges.

How we use it

Clients are sometimes prone to generalisations that distort what's going on. We hear them say, '*Everything's awful. I just can't do anything right. The whole world is against me.*' Their energy is drained; they are demotivated and may be caught in a vicious spiral.

The ground from which we work is a belief that everyone has strengths and has had some successes in the past. We ask, '*When did you do something like this well in the past?*' and '*What has gone well then?*' and ask them to acknowledge these successes by writing them over a star.

Then we move to the clouds and ask for specifics about what is challenging, encouraging clients to be really focused in what they write. We spend quite a long time clarifying an issue before it is ripe for recording.

Then we can move to ask clients which cloud they would like to dispel first.

Put it into action

This printed page is too formal for the organic conversations that characterise coaching and facilitation:
- Ask your client to draw the stars and clouds themselves.
- Use cut-out coloured paper shapes to write on with groups.

Stars and Clouds

Competence Ladder

What this is

The competence ladder is usually drawn as four steps, from unconscious incompetence to unconscious competence. It describes a series of predictable stages through which people pass as they learn something new. It is useful for tracking progress and confidence, and helping people stick with the discomfort of the conscious stages of learning. This discomfort happens when we know we can't yet do what we'd like to do, or we are doing it with ferocious concentration in order to get it right.

Our ladder recognises that learning is not a once-and-for-all journey: we may grow our competence and then find it diminishing or entering a new phase. The additional top step, mastery, identifies a high level of flow that we may consider very desirable, and which also signals the potential dangers of being beyond the rules or losing sight of the journey.

How we use it

We often use this in training. For instance, we:
- map out the steps on the floor
- ask participants to identify which step they are currently on in relation to their learning
- explore what it feels like to be on different steps
- find out what has helped them to move up the ladder in the past
- repeat the exercise at a later stage in the training.

We notice that on the first day, some participants may stand on the third step, only to move down a step later, when they realise that the thing they are learning is more complex than they had thought originally.

Put it into action

- Use the diagram, with or without walking about a space, to explore where clients are in a learning journey or in skills development.
- Recognise that people do slip back and lose confidence in their ability.
- Be alert for times when we ourselves become complacent.
- Ask yourself what else you might need to know, as things move on.

Competence Ladder

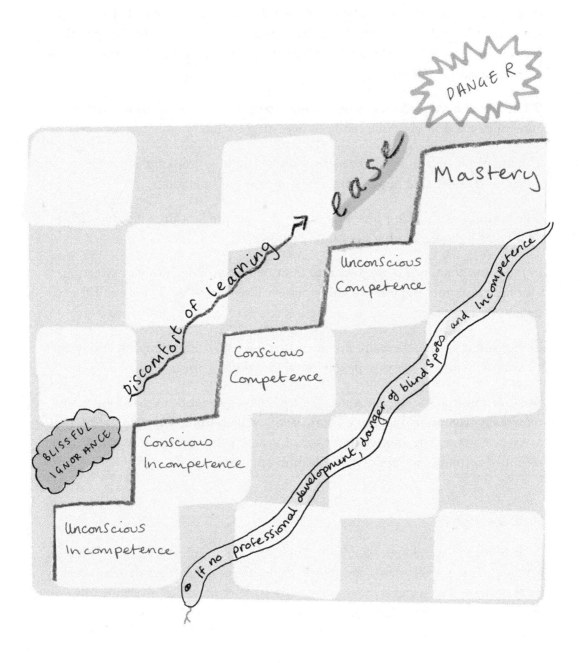

Comfort, Stretch, Panic in Learning

What this is

People who have done an analysis of their learning, personality or behavioural styles sometimes think that they must now adjust everything to fit the style they prefer. We've heard people say, '*I can't do that, I'm a visual learner. I need you to give me the information differently.*'

While we all have preferences and stronger suits in some skills than others, we are none of us fixed in only one mode of operating for life.

The image of *comfort, stretch and panic zones* is helpful in thinking about feelings in situations that demand new learning or new ways of operating.

One person loves making presentations to 500 people in a large hall and feels in their comfort zone; another goes into a panic.

In the panic zone, our brain goes into fight or flight mode. We start sweating. Our heartbeat goes up; our breathing gets shallower and faster. We can't think straight. We can't learn.

In the comfort zone, there are no challenges, no unsettling thoughts, and we can coast along without questioning anything. We don't learn much.

We learn most in the stretch zone. We are enabled to work in that zone when we already have a safe base, a comfort zone, to draw from, when we know how to keep the boundaries so we don't stray into the panic zone, and when we have identified resources to support us in learning new things.

How we use it

A client might be talking about how they avoid doing something that is difficult for them. Perhaps they have committed to doing something but then when they meet opposition, they give way. Perhaps they are reluctant to give someone feedback on behaviour that is having a negative impact on others.

Comfort, Stretch and Panic

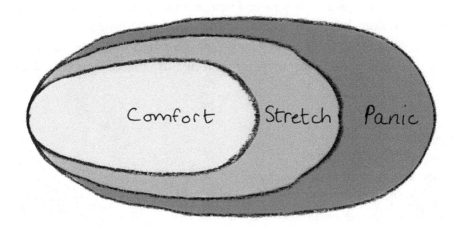

We ask them, '*How much of a stretch is this for you?*' and '*When have you done this sort of thing and felt comfortable?*' as a lead-in. If this line of questioning seems fruitful, we draw the diagram and explain it helps us think about what sort of things they prefer and how to expand their repertoire.

If a client comments that the comfort zone is small, we can draw a dotted line to extend this zone into the stretch zone, and ask them about their growing edge:
- How much do they want to grow?
- How could they extend the stretch zone to minimise panic?

See the next page to turn the model on its side and for detailed suggestions for putting it into action.

Put it into action

If you are working with a kinaesthetic learner or someone who likes moving around in a coaching session, you could mark out areas of the floor to represent comfort, stretch and panic, and also create a fourth space as the situation or context to which the client is reacting. Then suggest to the client that they stand in a place that reflects how they feel about the situation. You can stand beside them, which might lead to your picking up information from your physical proximity or shared perspective, or you might like to observe from a neutral place.

Try questions such as these:
- *What does it feel like there?*
- *Where would you be more comfortable?*
- *What is different when you stand elsewhere?*
- *How do you normally react to discomfort?*
- *If you stand in each of the three zones in turn, what happens?*
- *Where would your colleagues stand in relation to the situation?*
- *Where do you choose to stand now?*
- *What would support you?*

Alternatively, you could use small objects in conjunction with the diagram to represent the various players in the situation and ask the client to move them around:
- *Which object would represent you in this situation?*
- *Where would you be?*
- *Where would other people be?*
- *What would you see from their perspective?*
- *How could you get people to move?*

Stretch Stimulus

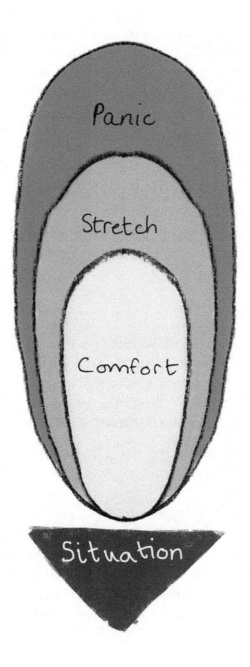

Dilts' Neurological Levels

What this is

Many people find this framework, frequently referred to as 'Dilts' Logical Levels', is a useful analytical tool. Studies in neuroscience now explain more about the workings of the brain, so you will meet other representations too. The proposition is that there are six different levels at which a person might be operating at any given moment, and impacting at the higher levels on the pyramid will have a deeper and more lasting transformational effect. The higher levels are seen to take you closer to the root cause; lower levels are more like symptoms:

- *I am on this earth to smoke* (Purpose)
- *I'm a smoker* (Identity)
- *I need to have a cigarette when I get stressed* (Belief)
- *I blow great smoke rings* (Capability)
- *I always smoke a couple of cigarettes after a meal* (Behaviour)
- *I want a cigarette when I'm in the pub* (Environment).

How we use it

Our understanding is that each of these levels is interconnected and the hierarchy is not absolute. Our experience is that hearing the level at which the client is thinking can help us to pitch our questions appropriately to unlock thinking. When we ask questions that take a client's thinking up the levels, we can help them both to have new insights into why they are stuck in a particular habit of mind or behaviour and subsequently to change.

Put it into action

Try consciously asking questions that address the next level up with clients and notice what happens. Taking an issue through each of the levels discretely helps your client untangle the various skeins in their knotted thinking so they see clearly for themselves where the most powerful lever for change is situated. You can also use the various levels systematically to help a team unstick and move forward.

Neurological Levels

Strengths Smiley

What this is

Focusing on and articulating what someone does well builds their confidence and enables them to put themselves forward for new learning. It helps to counter the all-too-common tendency to exaggerate the proportion of the negative to the detriment of the positive.

How we use it

Clients from many different walks of life want to boost their self-confidence or work on their skills and strengths. Sometimes they are wholly externally validated: that is, they only really believe they have done well and are good enough when another person tells them so. We may use this simple activity to boost a client's self-esteem, help them get an idea of their strengths when they are applying for jobs or build their internal self-validation muscle.

Put it into action

Using a smiley in a coaching session goes like this:
- Ask the client to draw a smiley face in the centre of a piece of paper, label it with their name and draw a number of lines coming out from the face, as though they are rays from a sun.
- Ask the client about things they do well or feel good about and suggest they write these things on the lines.
- Ask the client what someone else would say they do well and to write this down too.
- Ask about a situation where they felt pleased about what they had done and talk about the skills they used, etc.

Gradually, the amount of strength-based evidence on the page will build up to something that you can celebrate together and the client can take away as a visual reminder.

Strengths Smiley

Chapter 5

Leading, Influencing and Motivating

Leading, Influencing and Motivating

A client in a senior role in a large company asked recently how she could be more aware of her management style and hold to it in a way that inspired respect from her colleagues. She had been in this executive role for years and wanted to understand and articulate what leadership was for her. Managers transitioning to new roles ask similar questions. Whole leadership teams may question the way they behave and how they can influence others more effectively, particularly at times of organisational change and upheaval. We hope this chapter will help individuals and teams reflect on and develop vision, direction, style, cohesion and effective behaviour.

We have written out of our own experience as coaches of people in executive and management positions, as trainers in management skills, and as managers, leaders and employers ourselves. We offer a collection of models and images that have helped both us and our clients to unpick messes, see fresh perspectives, think differently and acquire new behaviours.

In the chapter, we use 'leader' and 'manager' almost interchangeably. We are aware of several classical definitions that may help people to think about their exact role in an organisation and how to play it out – and there are stacks of books on leadership and management already for that purpose.

The people we work with need to:
- establish aim and direction of the company/team/work (vision)
- plan how to get there (strategy, timelining, resourcing)
- align people to achieve a goal (communication, team building)
- deliver on agreements (motivation, coordination, solution finding)
- stay sane and healthy in complex contexts (balance, resilience).

They may be:

- in positions of status in a hierarchy, yet fear they lack influence
- exposed to public scrutiny and desiring greater confidence
- newly promoted and unsure how to proceed
- challenged by change and looking to motivate their teams
- seeking a companion to help them think and define a way forward.

Whatever the specifics of their context and need, they lead people. Others follow. They are influential models, sometimes consciously, sometimes not. They are involved in interactions with groups whom they may need to keep safe. And they want to take the people they lead on a journey, whose end destination they may or may not have clearly defined.

Use this chapter to develop your own or other people's awareness of their roles. Great leaders are able to live out their roles effectively, in line with their values and the needs of their organisations.

We include diagrams that relate to:

- understanding spheres of influence and concern in leadership
- determining vision, holding direction and getting there
- analysing where people are in the team
- choosing appropriate styles of intervention, consultation and leadership
- energising, motivating and problem-solving with colleagues.

Circles of Leadership

What this is

Overlapping circles, or Venn diagrams, can help us to focus on aspects of leadership, increasing impact and effectiveness. This particular model, the Action-Centred Leadership model, described by John Adair, has circles that show how the interests of the task, team and individual overlap in places, yet are also distinct. We, or our clients, may redraw this with larger/smaller areas of overlap and emphasis.

How we use it

We use this model to stimulate reflection, asking about three areas:
- the task or project the leader is delivering: its outcome, timescales, success criteria, resourcing
- the team engaged in delivering the task: its make-up, skills, report lines, strengths, development areas
- the client and their leadership role: skills, competencies, fears, hopes, communications, own reporting structures.

Separating out the various aspects and looking at how they interact helps to create clarity and new perspectives and enables thinking about values and goals, personal characteristics and influence, and the social nature and organisational context of leadership.

Put it into action

Look at the areas of intersection with your client, asking:
- *How do you interact with the team? Where are the tensions? Where are the opportunities? How might you influence differently?*
- *How do you interact with the project? To what extent are you fully signed up to its principles and objectives? Is it an end in itself or a stepping stone to professional development?*
- *How does the team interact with the project? What conflicts of interest are there? Who is vying for leadership? What might make this team deliver differently? How strong is commitment to the project?*

Circles of Leadership

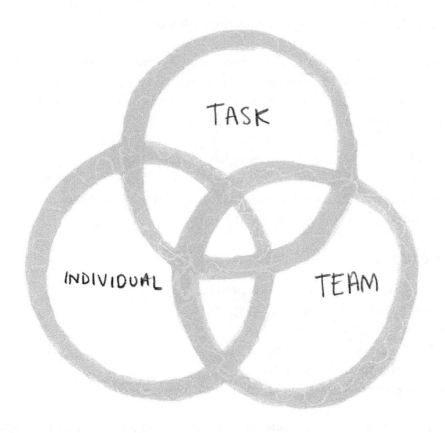

Maximised Energy

What this is

This diagram helps us to explore what we can do something about and what we can't do anything about. Then we can decide where to put our energy and where to let things go. All great things to consider with a client.

'*It's raining again,*' says a client. '*I'm anxious about the weather,*' using energy on an area of concern outside their control. '*I'm thirsty,*' says a client. '*I wish someone would bring some tea.*' This is within their control. They can ask someone to make tea or make it themselves.

If we spend a lot of our energy worrying about things that we can't control, we end up feeling powerless, anxious and overwhelmed. The sweet spot is where we focus our energy on the areas we can control. This is why we have called the centre of our diagram ME – Maximised Energy.

How we use it

We use this diagram with clients to explore:
- how they use their emotional energy
- how they might be more proactive
- how they can let go of worries
- what power for action they have
- how to grow their area of control.

We invite clients to write thoughts into one space or the other. This brain-dump activity can be really useful in itself for an overwhelmed executive! Together, we look at the balance and explore where their energy can be most effective.

We consider how different forces, actions or thoughts have the potential to extend or diminish the ME area. Then we ask our clients what they choose to do or think differently.

Maximised Energy

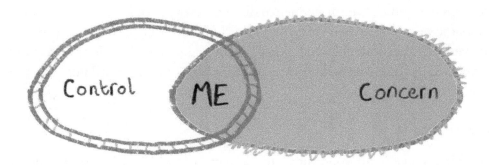

Put it into action

When a client appears to be concerned about lots of different issues, or is jumping around as they describe a situation:

- Ask that old favourite coaching question, '*Which bits of this do you have control over?*'
- Invite them to allocate all their concerns to an area of the diagram.
- Explore what they want to achieve.
- Explore with them what might grow their area of control.
- Ask them what they need in order to let go of things outside their control.
- Work with them on how to direct their energy to achieve this.

Spheres of Influence

What this is

These nesting circles extend the areas of influence and concern described above. We can use them to clarify how much influence we have, with whom and when. The degree to which we can influence different areas of our life and work varies, as does the degree to which different factors influence our perspectives and the way we make decisions. The individual occupies the central circle and has most control over themselves, with diminishing amounts of control or influence over the areas in the other circles.

How we use it

These circles give us an opportunity to pick up on some of the messages clients give themsleves about other people's control over them. When we hear a client talking about what this or that person says, we:

- ask if they would like to explore the impact of different influences and people on their thinking and behaviour
- offer this model to capture the strength of influence
- explore whether this is actually what the client wants
- decide what needs to change, in terms of thinking or action, to achieve what the client does want.

We ask clients to write their own name in the central circle and to label the other circles according to the relative degree of influence they have. The dialogue and the activity help them to:

- realise the extent to which they can, or cannot, influence others
- reflect on where their influence is direct or indirect
- be more realistic about what they aim for
- be more inventive in harnessing other people and resources to extend their influence further.

Put it into action

Draw the circles with the client, using as many circles as they like. Where does their strongest influnce come from? Work? Then that goes in the innermost circle. The family? The next band out. And so on, with categories that are meaningful to the client and the coaching context. These might include work, social circle, company, city, region, country, global market, etc.

Spheres of Influence

If clients exaggerate the demands of others or apparently dismiss the strength of certain influences, probe more deeply to unpack their thinking in that area more. Experiment with putting the circles in a different order. Ask, '*What does seeing it like that tell you?*'

The Leadership Journey

What this is

We created this diagram to help leaders and managers to talk about:

- where they are now in the development of their career
- transitioning from a task-oriented role to one focused on strategy
- what triggers the ups and downs in their experience of work
- identifying the next stage and how they might get there.

The undulating river represents the leadership journey. It is not a straight line from start to finish and there will be times when the traveller can't see what lies round the next bend. The bubbles suggest aspects of the landscape through which many people pass. You might connect these to Torbert's Seven Transformations model of leadership or Collins' Level 5 Leadership growth curve.

How we use it

We typically use a diagram such as this with people transitioning to new responsibilities or ambitious to move on and wondering what they need to prepare themselves for next. We ask them to:

- draw a line to represent their own career/promotion/leadership journey
- explore what was going on at the peaks and dips – and is going on now
- consider how different stages require a task or a relationship orientation
- label the curve with words/visuals that are relevant for them
- decide what to celebrate or simply accept about their past experience
- identify any behaviours/patterns/responses they might want to change
- decide where they want to go next in their career
- identify what learning will be useful for them on the way.

We endorse them for their competence/efficiency in one role and normalise their experience if performance and confidence have fallen off at times. This often happens as people acquire new roles, are expected to perform new tricks and fall under scrutiny from a new team as they do so.

Put it into action

Encourage creativity (scribble, bubbles, images, arrows, symbols, colour) as you explore:
- changes in self-perception
- reactions to change (imposed by others or self-initiated)

The Leadership Journey

- performance anxiety
- team responses
- conflicts, jockeying for power
- learning new skills and knowledge
- changes in organisational and personal circumstances.

Neurological Levels for Management Style

What this is

We created this adaptation of Dilts' Neurological Levels model (described in Chapter 3) with someone who wanted to develop their own management style. The model shows how the individual's beliefs about the world and work meet the pressures of the work context to influence an individual's choice of behaviour and managerial style. Unpicking all these aspects helps create insight into what's going on, and supports conscious choices about how to behave consistently, appropriately and with integrity.

How we use it

We use this model to help managers to identify and articulate principles that can guide their choices and shape their behaviour in response to their team and context. Someone might say:

- *I give clear direction; help the company and team succeed* (Purpose)
- *I think honesty, fairness, transparency are vital* (Values)
- *People need to help each other and to be safe to take risks* (Beliefs)
- *I want to be seen to be empathetic, encouraging, pragmatic* (Style)
- *I open up my meeting room to my team when I can* (Behaviour)
- *The office is crowded, open-plan and noisy* (Environment).

Put it into action

Sketch out a blank triangle with lines across it. Ask about:

- what's going on at the level of the environment – delineating the problem, issues, context in which the person works
- what the purpose of the individual's role is – through their eyes
- what values and beliefs they hold
- how they want to be seen by their team
- how they now choose to behave to embody their style and beliefs in the team and organisational context
- how to apply this awareness in future, in different contexts.

Neurological Levels for Management Style

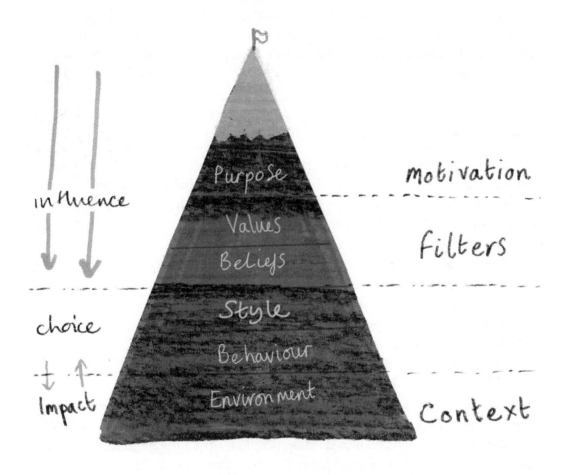

Contextual Leadership

What this is

The sketches opposite illustrate different styles of leading and interacting with your team. They are all appropriate in different contexts and all impact differently on the climate at work. Effective leaders and managers flex their style to suit the context and the people. Leaders who do this appropriately are likely to be the most successful.

How we use it

We use sketches like this to prompt exploration when clients want to work on their leadership style, for example when they are in transition to new posts, roles or companies, and are feeling their way in terms of what the prevailing culture is and how best to achieve their aims. We ask:

- *How does the company/team culture look to you?*
- *Where do you identify?*
- *How would you draw your own style of leadership?*
- *What's going on between your people at the moment?*
- *What do you want to achieve?*
- *What could you adjust to be more effective?*
- *What might trigger a change of style in the future?*

We might also point to the work of Daniel Goleman, which explores the contexts in which particular leadership styles are likely to be effective. A coaching style of leadership, for instance, is seen to develop people for the future and lead to long-term strength. This is not so appropriate in a crisis situation, when a leader might need to adopt a very directive style that demands immediate compliance. Hence the need to explore with our clients the context in which they are working, the needs of the situation and the outcome they want to achieve.

Put it into action

Offer some sketches to the client or create drawings together of different leadership styles in action. Reflect together on what the client sees in the drawings and what they imagine of the context in which these leaders are operating.

Leadership Styles in Action

Explore:
- what the climate at work is like for them
- what they hear people saying/see them doing
- whether everyone is like this
- what the needs of the organisation are
- what might work for them in this context
- what adjustments they will make themselves, with whom.

Leadership Style, Skill and Will

What this is

Our thinking here draws on Hersey and Blanchard's model of Situational Leadership. The starting principle is that leaders need to adapt their style with different people to get the most out of them. If you delegate a complex project to someone new in a post who doesn't yet have the skills or knowledge to carry it out autonomously, the chances of success are small.

We suggest four possible groupings of skill and motivation (will):
- entry-level skill, variable will
- low levels of skill, but high levels of will
- high levels of skill, but varying motivation
- high levels of both skill and motivation.

The diagram suggests a progression of leadership behaviours that are more or less supportive/directive, to suit staff levels of skill/will and career stage:
- Directing – giving clear instruction, and boundaries at entry level.
- Mentoring – expert guidance from someone who has been there.
- Coaching – encouraging, developing independence, keeping on track.
- Delegating – autonomy within parameters, touch points and review.

How we use it

We use this model when a client is looking for a more effective way of managing someone in their team. We ask if they are familiar with the model and if they would like to look at it. We explore how they see their team and individuals, and what they understand the different leadership styles to be. Then we ask how this might relate to the person they are worried about.

Put it into action

Use the diagram to help clients think about the team as a whole. Explore their view of the different levels of motivation in the team:
- *Who would they place in each quadrant of the table?*
- *How have they observed individuals responding to different styles?*
- *What might be worth trying?*
- *How exactly would they put their ideas into action?*

Leadership Style, Skill and Will

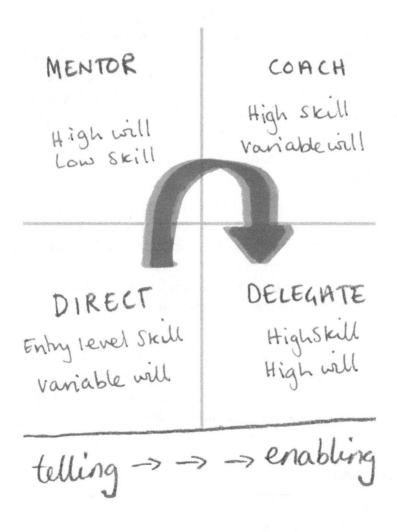

MENTOR

High will
Low skill

COACH

High skill
Variable will

DIRECT

Entry level skill
Variable will

DELEGATE

High skill
High will

telling → → → enabling

Hierarchies of Need

What this is

The concept of a set of needs that must ideally be met in sequence originates in the work of psychologist Abraham Maslow, around 1943, and has been developed and illustrated numerous times since. Maslow's original hierarchy has five levels. We have adapted it here. Others have adapted it too, so you may now see the hierarchy presented with seven or eight levels, including cognitive, aesthetic and transcendence needs. John Whitmore adds Legacy as his top level, noting that very senior leaders may want to explore the legacy they will leave when they have achieved what they want in the present job.

How we use it

Despite reservations today about the validity of the underlying concept, the original idea and resultant models can be a useful prompt when considering factors influencing motivation. Some clients see a link between their lack of motivation at work and an unmet need for recognition and status. Others say they are '*at the top*' and '*these are nice problems to have*'. Perhaps this is code for '*I know I am lucky*'. The client's response gives us ground for exploration.

People operating in the bottom two layers of the hierarchy are not likely to be whole, resourceful, capable, creative or fully present to work towards growth or change. Coaching is unlikely to be appropriate for them. And it may not always be possible or wise to coach someone who lacks comfort and balance at the third level – other types of support may be more useful.

Put it into action

Use this model to consider:
- what might be affecting behaviour and motivation
- how these factors interlink with where someone is on the Change Curve (described in Chapter 6)
- where, when and how to intervene to improve motivation
- how this model changes awareness of self and others.

Pyramid of Needs

No wonder people may seem less motivated when moving house; it's probably more than just the inability to find a favourite pair of socks!

Levels of Consultation and Decision Making

What this is

Despite extensive research, we do not know who created this model. On a stall at a Managing Change charity fair in 1997, it reached a colleague via a chain of unknown people. Many really useful models appear like this, created in a moment of exploration and then gaining a strong general application. We think it is based on Sherry Arnstein's Ladder of Citizen Participation.

'Consultation' has a different meaning for the decision maker (the star symbol) and the team members (the plain circles) at each level:

1   At level 1, the leader takes a decision and instructs the team on how to perform the task. Appropriate for dismissals and crises.
2   At level 2, the leader asks for input into a decision and then tells the team what they have decided. This is not really consultation.
3   At level 3, the team are active in discussion and consultation, but the leader is the person who ultimately takes the decision.
4   At level 4, the leader operates as part of the team on an equal basis. The decision is taken by consensus and everyone takes responsibility.
5   At level 5, the leader sets the parameters within which the team can operate, stands back, lets the team decide and accepts their decision.

How we use it

Problems often come when leaders and their reports have different understandings of how 'consultation' will play out in reality. We explain the points above then wait. Clients become totally absorbed, moving their fingers up and down the different levels as they analyse when they use a particular style and how appropriate it might be for the situation.

Put it into action

Ask your clients what consultation means for them/their team. Explore:
• *What sort of consultation might you want to use in this situation?*
• *What underpins that choice? What are the implications?*

Levels of Consultation and Decision Making

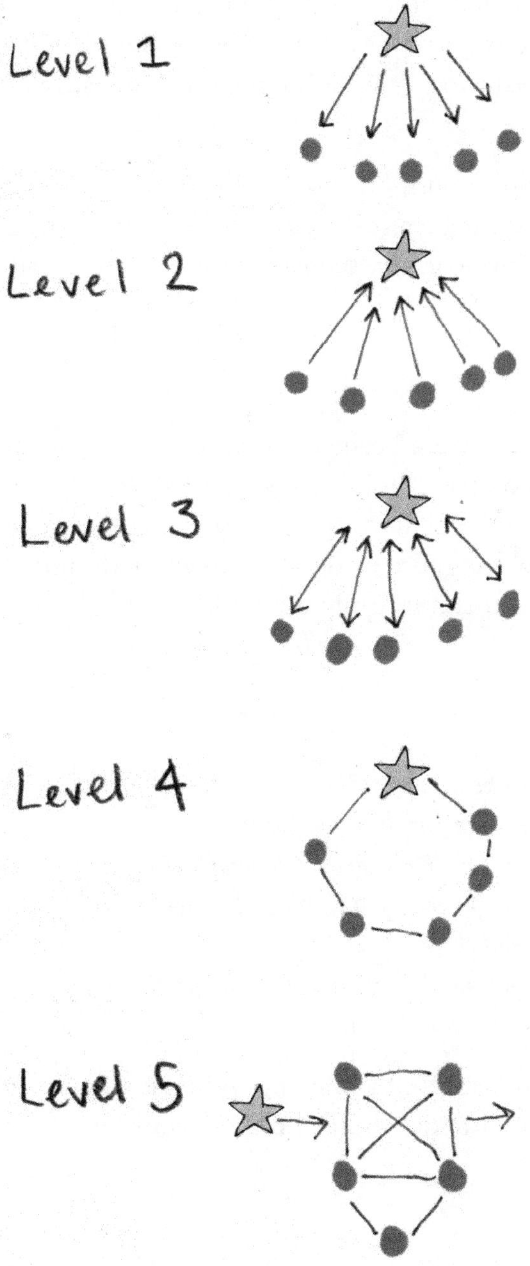

Level 1

Level 2

Level 3

Level 4

Level 5

True North

What this is

A compass helps people orientate themselves in the world. Where there is no clear path, the compass is a vital piece of kit. We use a compass to find true North, but it's just as useful if we want to head East, West or South. It depends where we start and where we want to go. What's important is to look at it often to keep on track.

Here's the relationship to business and life. In an uncertain world, there is often no predetermined path. It helps to clarify where we're starting from, where we'd like to get to. Coaching works in the gap between where you are now and where you want to be.

How we use it

We ask clients where they are headed in their career, company or life, and then suggest they draw a compass, with images or words for the destination, distractions and other influences. As they draw, they engage. We clarify: what's needed to help them focus; how to ignore or deal effectively with distractions; and what they will do to hold the destination firmly in mind.

Put it into action

Ask your clients:
- *What attracts you like a magnet?*
- *What sort of compass might help you get there?*
- *What would it look like if you drew this compass?*
- *What distractions might pull you in other directions?*
- *How could you avoid them?*
- *How often might you need to consult your compass?*
- *How could you ensure you do this?*

Or use a real compass instead of a drawing. And use the real thing or a drawing as an anchor, a personal reminder to stay on track yourself.

True North

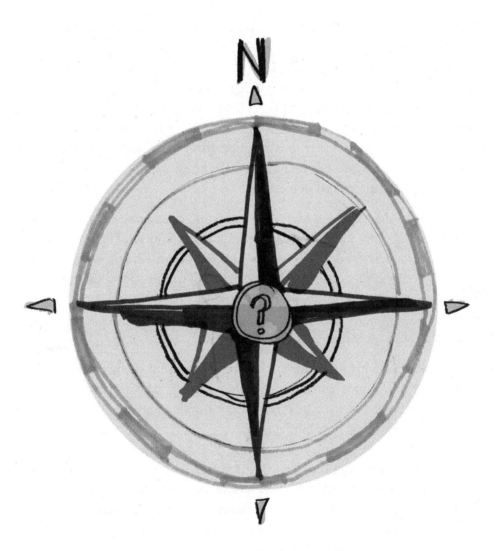

The Axis of Ego

What this is

We don't know where this diagram originates, but it is a quick and clear way of illustrating what often happens in meetings, negotiations and other decision-making discussions. It is played out in board meetings all over the world. When faced with a complex problem, we often start from the premise '*I am right*', which incorporates the construct that my idea, suggestions and solution to our problem are correct. If I am right, it follows that you (if you are contradicting my suggestion or offering a different solution) are wrong. Once we get to that position, it becomes a tug of war. Little cooperation or creative joint thinking is likely. It is now a win/lose conversation, which rarely supports either the individual or the organisational objectives.

The way out is to stop and consider what everyone does agree on and key criteria for deciding whether to adopt a particular solution or course of action. This impersonalises the conversation. Now the idea (or person) is not wrong; it just doesn't fit the criteria. It's easier to think clearly. Disparate views can converge, possibilities narrow and minds meet in agreement!

How we use it

We use the diagram with individuals who complain about disagreements with colleagues and with groups where there are conflicting ideas about how to go forward. Clients say it takes the heat out of their wish to promote their own idea without considering other possibilities. We:

- pause a win/lose repeating conversation
- refocus people on what they are jointly trying to achieve – ask '*What was the initial purpose you were trying to serve?*' '*What are your shared objectives?*'
- identify together one or more key criteria for measuring each suggestion against – ask how well each possibility meets the criteria
- confirm what the agreed solution is and ensure it is recorded.

Put it into action

Share this with clients who want to come to agreement more effectively for the common good. Or use it to help teams see the potentially destructive patterns of their discussions.

The Axis of Ego

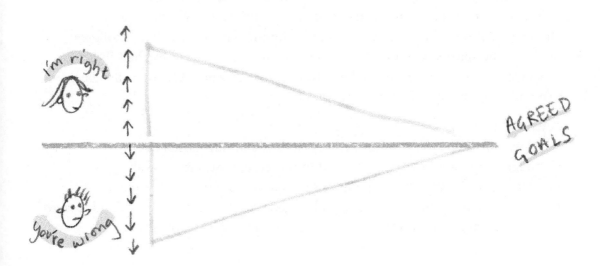

Here is a series of possible questions to ask groups working on joint decision-making:

- *What is the fundamental issue here?*
- *What sort of outcome are we looking for?*
- *What are the criteria for deciding on a particular course of action?*
- *What possible suggestions do we have?*
- *How well does each match our criteria?*
- *How else might we measure success?*
- *How will we remember what has been agreed?*

Support Challenge Matrix

What this is

As we work with colleagues or clients, we want to find the mix of approaches that calls them to their best. This matrix maps the combination of support and challenge that is vital for motivation and optimum performance. Think of great teachers who spurred you on to exceed your own expectations by their judicious mix of stretch and care. And maybe there were some who were so challenging that you were hardly able to perform at all.

We think that:
- low support + low challenge lead to inertia and disengagement
- high support + low challenge lead to missed opportunities for all
- strong challenge + low support raises anxiety, undermines confidence
- high support + high challenge lead to great results for both the individual and the organisation – it is the only combination to raise energy.

How we use it

We typically use this when we notice leaders talking with disappointment about other people's performance and the need to motivate their team. We offer them this matrix and ask them to analyse the approaches they are using with various people. Then we invite them to consider the responses they receive and how they could adapt their approach.

Put it into action

Use this model with people who are dissatisfied with how they are managing or motivating their line reports or colleagues:
- Ask them what they want to be different.
- Get them to map their people into the boxes according to how much they support or challenge them.
- Explore what they need to do to get the right mix of challenge and support with everyone they work with.

Support Challenge Matrix

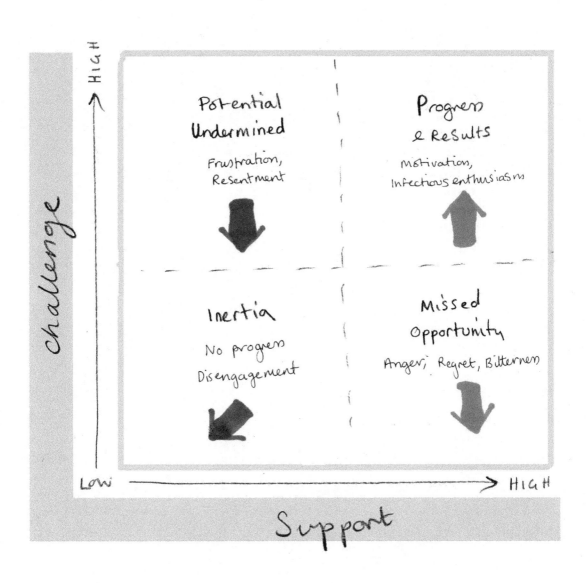

Chapter 6

Analysis, Choice and Change

Analysis, Choice and Change

In this chapter, we explore the territory that is probably the main working domain of Organisational Development leaders, Learning and Development professionals, and coaches. *Change.*

Like death and taxes, change is certain to come our way. All we know about most working contexts and organisations is that they have changed in the past, are changing now and will change in the future. '*Change or die*' we say, and '*Change is the only constant.*' Professionals in these fields want to manage, monitor, record and learn from change. We hope to avoid random, uncontrollable, chaotic change and aspire to a nirvana of planned, developmental, engaging, seamless transition!

The thing we most want for people we work with is that they should be at choice, rather than drifting and at the mercy of processes and forces they have not understood or even noticed. Those of us who have enough of the world's good things always have a choice, even if it is only whether to smile or not, whether to speak, whether to get out of bed or not. So in the title of this chapter, we sandwich choice between analysis and change. A skilled professional hopes to analyse the situation, organisation, market or context, identify shifts and trends, and respond from a choice of possible changes.

So here we bring together models that identify, explore and record change in a variety of ways and contexts. We've changed some diagrams that originated elsewhere. And some are our own, which perhaps you will change in your turn to be more relevant to your work.

We consider change as a process for which we can plan. We discuss tools for the analysis that precedes effective decision making and planning. We move on to consider how people and organisations respond to changes, whether they be external or internal. And some of our models contain possibilities for monitoring the progress of your plans as you implement them.

There are also models in other parts of the book that are relevant to the arena of choice (for instance, any form of the learning cycle, described in Chapter 4).

And in one sense, this whole book is about responding to change, as we model and explore the processes of the people we work with and use the synergy of our connections to create and learn. We have developed the models in this book in synergy with and in response to clients and colleagues. Both the models and the ways in which we understand and explain things have evolved and changed as we have been affected and influenced by others. So, *thank you* to everyone who has described your world and your interpretations to us en route.

We include a mixture of well-known and original models. Some are particularly useful when working with groups. We include models for:
- thinking of options
- prioritising
- understanding competing forces in the organisation
- scaling and reviewing progress
- understanding and working with change.

Mapping our Thinking

What this is

Long ago, we used something we called *spidergrams* to map our thinking. Then Mind Maps were popularised by Tony Buzan soon after! Both are diagrams that help you to work out from a central idea to create a web of associations that you can later turn into a plan, if you want to. This non-linear approach helps to generate more ideas and connections in a free-flowing, non-judgemental way. A linear list may freeze the mind because of the unspoken assumption that there is a correct order. The underlying *'ought to'* makes it more difficult to think. Deciding on order is more effective when you have mapped the field. Tony Buzan's work has been the starting point for many people. There are now great programmes for mind mapping electronically too if you like technology.

How we use it

We use Mind Maps for ourselves, individual clients and groups. For example, to plan a meeting, we:
- put the focus in a circle in the middle of a sheet of paper
- draw lines out from the circle for the themes we want to address
- add smaller lines coming off the themes for linked ideas and details
- work in the order that seems right at the time
- circle, underline, colour or highlight words, and add images
- use the diagram as an aide-memoire, to help us follow the flow of the conversation organically and still cover all we want to.

Put it into action

If you are facilitating a training or team event, use a Mind Map to:
- gather your initial ideas of the content
- brainstorm ideas in small groups
- visualise possibilities for the team
- generate discussion about dreams, realities and priorities
- choose and discard options.

Mapping our Thinking

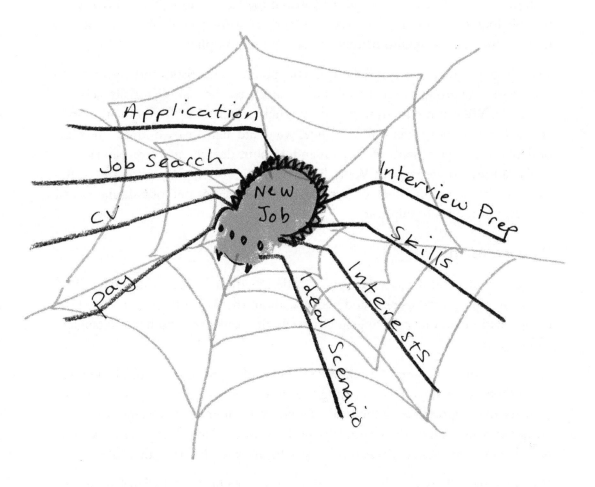

InVENNted Venns!

What this is

You may have come across Venn diagrams in maths at school. They show the possible logical relationships between sets and are named after John Venn, a nineteenth-century English mathematician and philosopher.

Venn diagrams help us identify both overlapping characteristics and aspects that are true of one group or set though not of another. They are pictorially very accessible. We can use them to plot how much groups (sets) have in common and how much they differ – for instance, we could analyse a workforce in terms of different groups of staff: those with and without degrees and professional qualifications. Some standard Venn diagrams show overlapping circles of equal size, such as the one in Chapter 5 that depicts the relationship of task, individual and team in the leadership role.

How we use it

Our invented Venn diagrams are purpose-designed for an individual client. They show something very specific and personal about the parts of a person's world or preoccupations and help us to gain clarity about areas that are otherwise tangled and unclear.

When someone talks about competing or interlinked aspects or work or life, we invite them to create a Venn, naming the circles and varying their size to show their relative importance or the relative amount of brain space or emotional energy they use. Thus, the example opposite was invented to explore how much of a client's mental energy was spent on/with the key players in their life.

When we have drawn circles that represent the current state of affairs, we ask the client what size they would ideally like the circles to be in relation to each other and how they might start to adjust them. We combine open questions with a visual comparison. The personalised Venn gives the client a measure for progress.

Put it into action

- Notice if someone describes competing areas of experience/endeavour.
- Offer the possibility of making the relative demands visual: '*I hear you talking about three interconnected areas of your experience: how might that look as a Venn diagram?*' or '*Could you represent that as three overlapping circles?*'

An inVENNted Venn

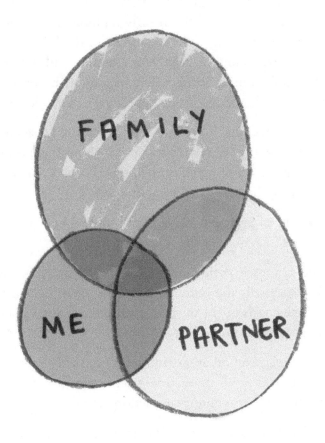

- Suggest drawing a Venn diagram, talking about the relative sizes of the circles as you go.
- Explore: *How does that seem to you? Does it feel as though the overlap is accurate here? Tell me about the different sizes of the circles. How else might it be? How would you like it to be? How might you start moving it?*

The Balance Wheel

What this is

This is an interactive circle often called the 'Balance Wheel' or the 'Wheel of Life'. Many coaches come across this in early training as a tool for helping clients explore their satisfaction with different areas of the life. Anyone can use it to chunk down big areas; consider relative importance, impact or progress; and establish starting points and prioritise. The measurement, or scaling, is generally most effective when done using a gut level of knowledge.

In its early forms, the wheel may have associations with life coaching rather than with, say, executive coaching. We're a bit sceptical about these distinctions: in our experience, clients always bring all of themselves to the coaching eventually! It's a very adaptable tool that can fit all sorts of needs.

We describe some general principles for using the wheel in coaching then outline examples of the wheel in action on the following pages.

The Balance Wheel is a circle divided into segments that each represent an aspect of life or work. It is generally the client who defines what the segments represent, though sometimes the coach might suggest areas to scale, as an analytical tool before the coaching starts, or in the first session.

The client indicates their level of satisfaction with each area:
- centre point = 0/10 = zero satisfaction; zilch; rubbish
- outer edge = 10/10 = maximum satisfaction; could not be better.

This scaling forms the basis of a conversation about which areas to focus on and the changes the client would like to work on. They may indicate level of satisfaction by drawing a line across the segment or by filling part of it in. Clients who process creatively may like to experiment with shape and colour, maybe shading in a section in a different colour each time they record progress.

Blank Balance Wheel

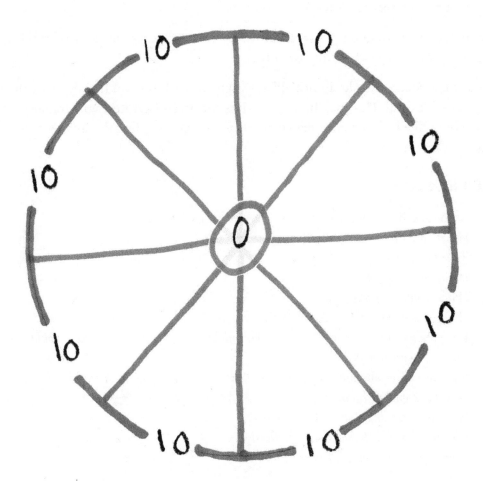

Scaled Balance Wheel

How we use it

We use the wheel sparingly, when it seems appropriate to help someone decide which of many pressing issues to focus on.

We prefer clients to define the segments themselves, because it helps keep the ownership of the agenda firmly with them.

In our experience, people do not always want to work first on the area that they have scaled lowest. This may be because it is the area of greatest vulnerability, and they would like to build confidence and trust by focusing first on an area that presents more hope.

Put it into action

After someone has scaled the wheel, ask questions such as:
*   *What occurs to you as you look at your wheel?*
*   *Talk me through your wheel.*
*   *What surprises you?*
*   *What would you like to work on?*
*   *What makes you score it X already?*
*   *If money (or any other segment the client might choose) were at 10, how would the other segments change?*
*   *If friendship (or any other segment the client might choose) were at 0, how would the other segments change?*
*   *How are these different levels connected?*
*   *Which could you change most effortlessly?*
*   *How would you like your wheel to look?*

A client once described their completed wheel as '*the cobweb of life*'!

Scaled Balance Wheel

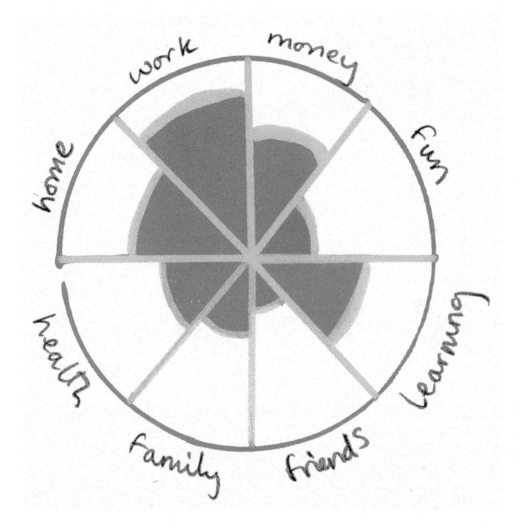

Wheel of Work

How we use it

We use a wheel of work on an individual or team basis. We invite people to create a wheel that is relevant to their situation and priorities. If they are stuck for areas, we brainstorm possibilities:

- stimulation
- organisational culture
- relationships with colleagues
- challenge of role
- level of responsibility
- support
- remuneration
- development opportunities
- career prospects
- match of values
- conditions
- benefits
- well-being
- peace of mind
- power and influence
- status
- recognition.

Working with an organisation, we define the wheel with the client teams, or with human resources or organisational development staff. We ask individuals or groups to scale the same categories as each other, compare scores, then explore the implications for the team and the organisation.

Remember: *an unbalanced wheel rolls neither far nor fast.*

Wheel of Work

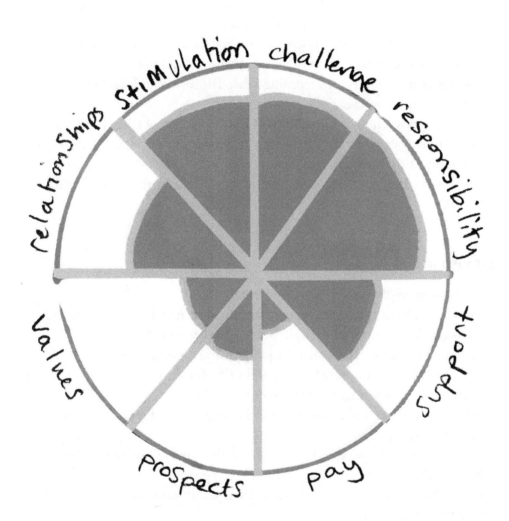

The Developmental Wheel

What this is

Our developmental wheel, with three concentric circles, has the scope for someone to use extra layers to plan forward and set goals:

- Each segment represents a potential area for balance in someone's life or work, and a potential area for development or coaching.
- The outermost ring is for recording what 10/10 would look like in each area – the outcome the client is moving towards.
- The innermost circle is for scaling. Mark the spokes of the wheel at even spaces to support scaling. Write 0 at the centre and 10 at the point where the spokes meet the next circle out.
- The middle ring is for recording a few steps to move the client towards 10/10.

Put it into action

Here's how you might use the developmental wheel:

- Ask the client to label the segments and record their level of satisfaction with each area in the innermost circle (see the earlier scaled wheel).
- Reflect together on the visual image, priorities and balance.
- Ask the client to choose where to focus first for development or coaching.
- Now work on the wheel one segment at a time.
- Ask what 10/10 would look like for this segment and record this in the outcome area.
- Explore what steps to take to move from the current position to 10/10.
- Record these in the next steps area of the segment.
- Discuss whether to move on to another segment now or to explore how to take the chosen steps.
- Continue the work on other segments of the wheel.
- Ask the client to develop this work further independently.

Developmental Wheel

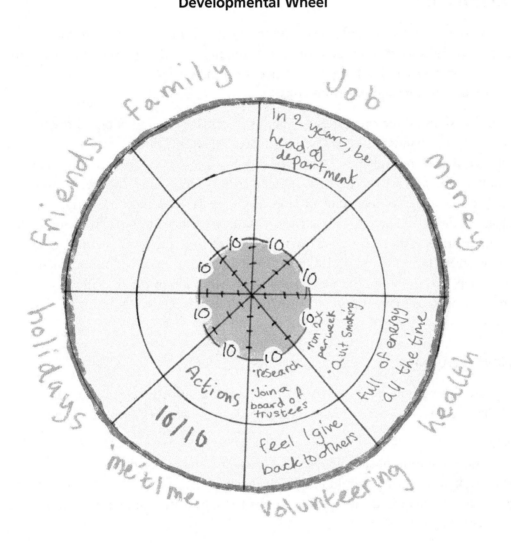

Do-It Disc

What this is

Apparently President Eisenhower used to organise his desk to separate the important tasks from the urgent ones. He sought to do the important rather than the urgent. So there is a long precedence for using relative urgency and importance to sort and prioritise tasks.

Our disc shows three categories to help us prioritise tasks and choose how to respond to demands. The shadow fourth area represents the essential space we all need to rest, restore and resource ourselves. Category A tasks are important and have the potential to influence organisational success and culture. B tasks are pressing and also important. B tasks may be delayed A tasks, now right up against a deadline, such as a tax return. C tasks take their urgency from someone else's priorities rather than your own. Too much time spent on B and C tasks causes stress, burnout and death! Their urgency leads us to crisis management and knee-jerk reactions. Staying on the right-hand side of the disc allows us to focus on what is most important and to resource ourselves to do it for the long term.

How we use it

We use this with people who complain about time poverty and overwork. It challenges how they are really working and how much they want to change.

We:
- ask them to populate the disc with their own tasks/activities
- look at what they would like to change
- support them in deciding how to sort tasks, prioritise and communicate their choices with others.

With groups, we mark out a large space with tape, invite people to stand where they think most of their activity takes place and ask what the positions feel like. This leads to support, exploration, hilarity, new ideas and collaboration. It also leads to agreements about team practices.

Do-It Disc

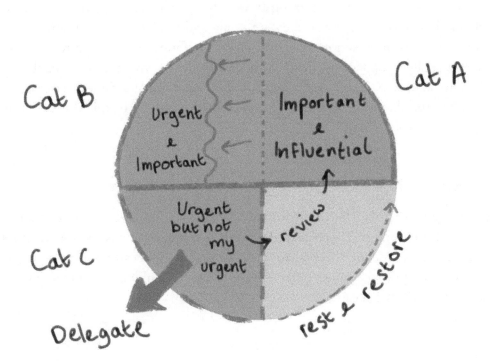

Put it into action

- Listen out for complaints about no time/too much work/late hours/anxiety about getting through things/overwhelm.
- Share the concept that tasks have relative importance, differing potential to influence and varied ownership.
- Explore people's habits, assumptions, options and choices.
- Identify what they will change and how to do it.

Review Pentagon

What this is

Many people like diagrams that are not square! We first met a pentagon like this on a course about Building Learning Power. It provides a framework for teams and individuals to analyse what they are doing and to make decisions about what sort of processes or behaviours to continue in the future. People can rotate it so different areas are uppermost first, altering the order in which they think about things, to suit them. There is less implied judgement about a right or correct order, and this degree of flexibility or control tends to help people think in a more relaxed and creative way.

How we use it

We have come across a lot of organisations asking staff to give feedback about their managers and other aspects of the business under headings such as the ones on our diagram. We use this pentagon rather than a list because the shape is more inviting and it produces more ideas and more lateral thinking. It is fun as a cut-out pentagon on coloured card!

Put it into action

When you are working with someone who is intent on reaching a particular objective, you may find that they are very keen to talk about all the extra things they need to do in order to reach their goal, without realising that they may also have to let go of something or alter their approach somewhere else if they want to fit everything in. Here's an opportunity to use the pentagon!

- Reflect back to them that you have heard about all the new things they intend to do.
- Ask them how feasible it is to carry on with everything else in the same way as they do now if they add in all these new actions.
- Ask, '*So what might you do more of/less of/let go of?*' '*And what do you want to keep?*'
- Challenge them on realism, commitment and detail of how they are going to change, maintain or let go of the behaviours they identify.

Review Pentagon

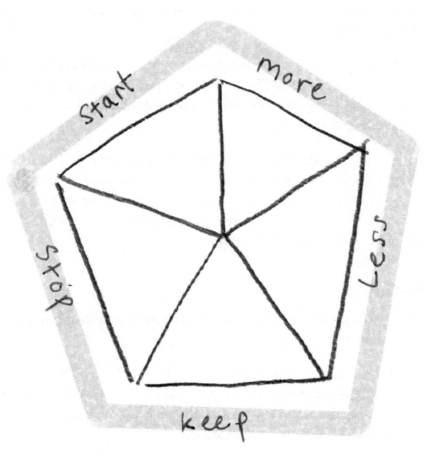

SWOT

What this is

Back to squares again! Leaders, consultants and students have used this diagram for many years as a quick and simple approach to analysing the position of a business in its market or competitive context.

The top two squares relate to the internal environment – for example, overheads, people and intellectual property. The bottom two relate to the external environment – for example, competitors, fashion and the law. The left-hand side is positive and the right negative.

It is common to create individual SWOTs for different aspects of a business in order to capture all the data. So a business may ask a wide range of people to contribute to SWOTs on product, process, market, logistics, finance, administration, etc. Individuals and teams can populate the boxes with their perceptions of the market and their business.

How we use it

We use this to help people capture all their understanding of their business's situation and prospects in one place.

We also use it for other aspects of people's lives. We might invite someone thinking of moving house to explore the pros and cons using a SWOT matrix. Seeing their whirring thoughts caught in categories helps them to work out which parts are within their control and which are not.

Put it into action

- Offer a SWOT when people are trying to capture lots of disparate influences on a situation.
- Be creative. Use it for varied situations and decision-making processes, not just business analysis. Experiment with a large space or coloured highlighters to refine the exploration.
- Allow time. This can be a work in progress for days.

SWOT

Basic SWOT

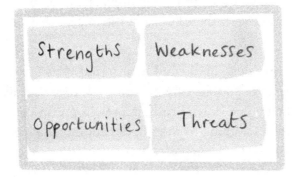

Positive/Negative SWOT

Internal/External SWOT

Force Field Analysis

What this is

Essentially, this simple diagram helps people disentangle the pressures that are affecting their work context or their lives and the impact that these pressures are having.

The horizontal line represents the desired state an individual or group is working towards. This may be an even state of equilibrium. It may be a dynamic smooth motion forwards. The up and down arrows represent pressures that depress or lift the line. When the forces coming from each direction balance each other out, the line stays on an even keel.

How we use it

We use this to identify what clients want as well as to explore what might help or hinder them in getting there. When we ask, '*So if we were to draw a line here, how close would that be to what you wanted?*' clients seize the pen and show us what it looks like for them. We ask questions about detail, change, time or measurement to expand our understanding before exploring what is influencing the situation and the impact of those influences. Then we move on to what is exerting most pressure and what the client can control or mitigate. This in turn leads to shifts of awareness and choice of action.

Put it into action

- Ask your client to draw a line representing how they want their life or their business to be.
- Find out why the line is where it is on the page.
- Suggest brainstorming to identify the pressures that impact, writing each pressure on a Post-it.
- Explore how much force and impact each item exerts, moving the Post-its around on the page together as you do so.
- Ask hypothetical questions: '*So what could you influence?*' '*So what would happen to your line then?*' '*So what might you change?*'

Force Field Analysis

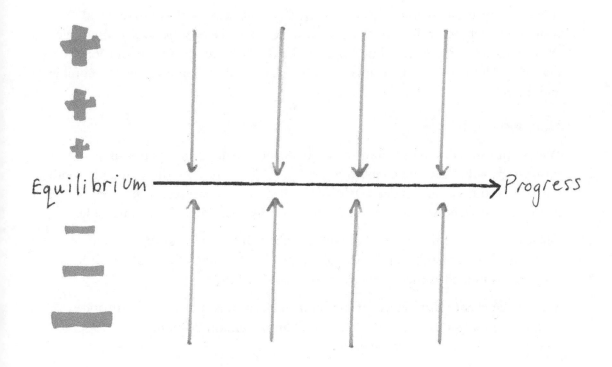

Futures-Based Planning

What this is

This diagram helps business owners create plans that relate to their overall vision and the values that they want to run through their business. It identifies various strands of the business and helps people think about these both separately and in relation to each other. It leads to an achievable sequence of steps so that timescales are manageable. The essential headings in the diagram are the Vision and Values headings. All the others are adaptable to the client and the context in both number and focus.

How we use it

We use this structure most often with directors of small businesses planning business growth. First, we establish when we are working to – the year and month we will see this vision achieved. We ask what the client will see, hear and notice in various aspects of the business so the vision is as clear as possible.

Then we ask about the values that will run through the business. We note that values are often identified and then submerged by the press of critical issues: here, they are positioned as the backbone of business growth.

We ask the client what aspects of the business need to be considered – finances, staff, resources, goods, services, clients, buildings, communication, technology – and create columns for each aspect.

As we work, we:
- offer a choice of who does the writing (when we do, clients appear to think faster)
- use individual sheets of paper for each section of the diagram
- work in chunks, checking out on how we are doing as we go
- ask the client to reflect on the emerging plan between sessions
- review thinking as we take up the threads again before moving on.

Put it into action

- If the client wants to work on a 20-year vision, beware! The planning could take so long that you might both run out of steam on the way.
- Offer the client different-coloured paper for each area: vision, values and each aspect they want to develop.
- Put the relevant year on each sheet of paper.
- Reorganise, cross out, tear up and start again until the plan looks right.

Futures-Based Planning

YEAR X	5 Year Vision				
	Services/ Goods	Clients	Values	Resources /Staff	Marketing
X – 1					
X – 2					
X – 3					
X – 4					
X – 5 = this year					

Transition Slice

What this is

Over years of working with people in change and development, we have noticed that in planning change, we often expect to go from one state or system to another without any transitional stage. It's as though we believe we can make huge changes without allowing any time for adjustment, experimentation and acceptance.

This model focuses on the interim period between one state or operating system, role or behaviour and another. At one side of the rectangle, we have the old; at the other, the new. The transition could be from experienced Head of Department to effective Executive Board member, or from running a tried-and-tested software system to full technical functionality with a new one. In the middle of the rectangle, we show the gradual shift of activity and focus from one state to the other, the decrease of the old order and the gradual growth of the new way of being. We have to actively understand and work to reduce the old patterns and increase and develop the new.

How we use it

We use this to prepare people and organisations for new roles, systems and structures. And we use it with individuals as they make the transition and struggle with their own and other people's habits and habitual expectations.

We sketch the model, discuss it and offer people the opportunity to populate it with what they are letting go of or leaving behind and what they are moving towards or adding. Sometimes people express this vocally; sometimes they write on the slice; sometimes we walk it out symbolically across a space.

We ask about strategies, support systems, communication, commitment, timescale and mindsets. Then we ask, '*So what needs to happen now?*'

Transition Slice

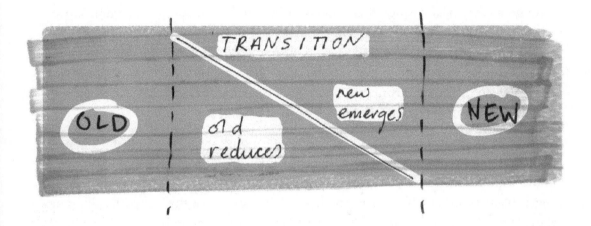

Put it into action

One of the best questions a fitness instructor can ask a new member of a gym is, '*What will you have to give up to work out as often as you suggest?*' Most people have thought about going to the gym, say, three times a week. Few have thought about what they will have to give up for that to happen.

Share the model:
- Discuss the transition.
- *Where are they now? And where do they want to be?*
- Check previous transitions and what has worked.
- Ask what the period might look like from other people's perspective.
- Discuss possible sticking points: *What might help overcome these?*
- Explore how to order and prioritise during the transition.
- Acknowledge that there will be a settling-in period.
- Consider how to make it smooth, real and effective.

The Change Process

What this is

This model draws on work by Elisabeth Kübler-Ross on the stages people go through as they deal with grief and news of impending death. The diagram shows reaction to change as a journey. There are typical staging posts, which people reach at their own pace, depending on their frame of mind and the degree of support or challenge they receive on the way. With appropriate time, support and challenge, we can move from resistance, which disables us, to acceptance, which frees us for action and energises us.

Various versions of this model are widely used in business. The graph starts at a point of stability, the status quo. A change is introduced. Initially, people do not know what to do. Then they often reject the change fiercely and express their anger, blaming others. If this has no effect, they bargain, in the hope of stalling or alleviating the impact. When they understand that the change is certain, they may become depressed and lose all energy. With support, they emerge to test out and finally accept the new reality.

How we use it

We use this with people who are leading initiatives, heading up a new team and struggling to understand reactions to their leadership, or are angry and resentful themselves about change in their lives. We:
- ask if they are familiar with the change curve
- offer the diagram and give a light-touch explanation, if appropriate
- ask how this might help their thinking; explore what comes up.

Put it into action

Suggest drawing separate lines for each individual in the team to stimulate reflection on the pace at which people go through the change process. Ask:
- *What has helped some people move more quickly than others?*
- *How have you responded differently to different individuals?*
- *What supported you at a similar stage on a change journey?*

The Change Process

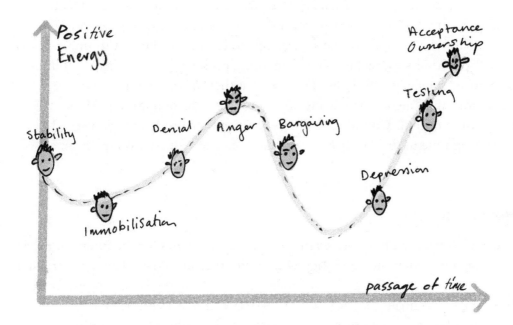

Differing Pace Within the Team

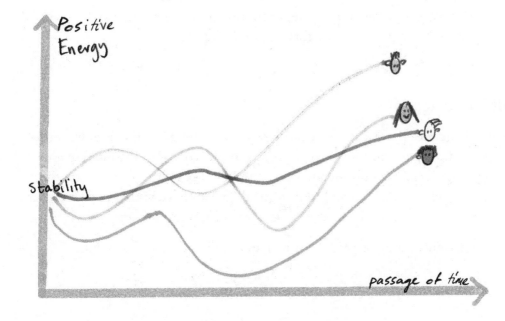

Change Analysis

What this is

Inspired by de Bono's *Six Thinking Hats*, we created this tool to help teams and individuals think through a change process in a systematic, rigorous way. We notice that when change is imposed, people often find it difficult to think clearly about opportunities or acknowledge anything positive, because there is leakage from unacknowledged feelings. The fear that their needs will not be met stops them from thinking constructively about strategies for minimising risk or maximising benefit. Considering different aspects separately aids clarity and dedicating time to feelings helps people to concentrate better on other aspects.

How we use it

We have often used this with teams. We agree guidelines for the interaction, encouraging participants to engage with each other in a coach-like manner, asking open questions, listening non-judgementally and accepting others' points of view. We explain the images and say we will work with one at a time:

- black/white exclamation mark = facts, evidence-based, unadorned
- gold star = good points, strengths, things that are going well
- red heart = feelings, the whole spectrum
- amber light = what might make us proceed with caution
- green leaves = signs of new life, opportunities open before us
- blue river = a positive flow forward to the future.

Put it into action

With a large group, treat this as a carousel activity. Establish the facts with the whole group. Split into four smaller groups. Each works on one discrete aspect: good points, feelings, cautions and opportunities. They then move to another group's flip chart, read and add to it, until all groups have visited each flip chart. You can then move to planning in whatever grouping you want.

With individuals, use postcard-sized images to hold and move around.

Change Analysis

	FACTS Black + White	
	GOOD POINTS Gold	
	FEELINGS Red	
	CAUTIONS Amber	
	OPPORTUNITIES Green	
	PLANS Blue	

Climbing the Mountain: Monitoring Progress

What this is

This is definitely one to draw with the client in the moment, rather than to bring in printed form. In essence, the image of the mountain is a tool for scaling and for measuring progress. It also helps people plan resources and gather strength and confidence for the next stage. The peak of the mountain represents someone's goal. The base of the mountain is their starting point. Climbing a mountain offers the opportunity of new views and perspectives opening up. Pausing on the climb helps people recognise and celebrate distance travelled – all things that a busy executive may not have time to reflect on enough in the midst of a pressured job and clamouring demands.

How we use it

We use this image with people who are feeling challenged by a big project such as cultural change. We ask, '*If you were to think of this project as climbing a mountain, where would you be now?*' They sketch the mountain and a figure, part way up. Then we ask questions such as:

- *So what has helped you get to this point already?*
- *What can you see now that you couldn't see before?*
- *What's going to help you get to the next stage?*
- *What's it going to be like when you get to the top of the mountain?*
- *How can you paint the benefits of reaching the top to the team?*
- *What might lie beyond this peak?*

Put it into action

Notice the sort of language your client is using. If they say they are '*stuck in the mud*' or find that getting the team on board is '*an uphill struggle*', using kinaesthetic language, this image is likely to be useful. When you offer it to a client, be alert to how actively they are responding and whether it is worth elaborating. Your client might like to draw in other members of the team, baggage that they have jettisoned on the way, a stick to lean on, a rucksack of provisions or even the next range of hills.

Climbing the Mountain

Chapter 7

Supervision and Team Facilitation

Supervision and Team Facilitation

Why have we grouped supervision and team facilitation together? We started writing about supervision on its own and realised that while supervision is of huge value to coaches, and also to practitioners in the helping professions, there are models and diagrams that can transfer to other areas. We hope that unchaining the models from one specific context will encourage you to experiment.

Facilitators help groups to reflect, discuss, learn and grow in relation to a specific project or issue. Team builders help groups to reflect on individual and collective interactions, purpose and organisational context – so that they come together to be more than the sum of their disparate parts. Supervisors help coaches and other practitioners to reflect on themselves and their work in the service of their clients, working on a 1:1 or group basis.

Facilitators, team builders and supervisors all work at the edge as they stimulate reflection, learning and growth. A company looking for someone to carry out any of these roles could have an internal cadre or could contract with a professional from outside. Someone external brings fresh eyes and runs less risk of colluding with the prevailing culture or of being undermined by conflict of interests. Someone internal costs less and knows the systems already. Whether internal or external, they need to:
- create a safe space for support and challenge
- be aware of the whole person and group/systemic dynamics
- hold the focus
- contribute knowledge
- bring creativity and lightness; rigour and strength
- be fully present in the moment.

Working with groups and teams

A group is not always a team. For instance, a group of coaches from disparate backgrounds may come together for supervision, each in pursuit of their individual objective. A team coalesces when a group of individuals in relationship work together to deliver a specific task, fulfil a function within a business or deliver a particular project, with mutual accountability. Building the team may be the leader's task – and it may be aided by facilitated events, focused on building understanding and relationship. Team facilitation, which is also event-based, looks at what is going on in the team with a resulting impact on how it operates and thus on how it achieves the task. Team coaching starts with a shared contract about the objective, takes place over time, and considers team process, task, systemic involvement and collective learning.

A word about supervision

Professionals in a number of fields benefit and grow through supervision. It is a safe and supported place to reflect on your practice and grow. Many people now find it an invaluable part of their professional infrastructure and it may also be required by a company or insurer. Many coaches have both individual and group supervision. Individual work ensures that we rigorously reflect on our own practice and are helped to notice patterns, skills and areas for growth. It is often a space for deep exploration at the point where the personal impacts the professional. Group work gives us additional perspectives, creates synergy and offers insights into a greater range of experience and techniques. Participants experiment with different approaches, observe others working, and have a chance to give and receive coaching, feedback and supervision in a spirit of mutual support and learning.

Models in this chapter are a stimulus for generating ideas and thinking about:
*   choosing a professional to work with
*   the facilitated learning/supervision process
*   the focus of our work
*   identifying where we are going as a team
*   looking at differences in a group or team
*   working together to win–win.

How to Choose a Facilitator, Coach or Supervisor

What this is

The marketplace is full of highly competent professionals. It's worth reflecting on which criteria carry most weight for us before we make a decision. This diagram helps with the choice. Each corner of the triangle represents a set of criteria that contribute to the decision.

Qualifications etc. cover professional profile, length of experience, level of skill, accreditation and how the person attained their qualifications.

Practicalities and logistics include: cost, location and proximity, availability, timings, Internet connections, and other probably unchangeable factors.

And the apex of the triangle, *personal characteristics and style*, is likely to be the deciding set of criteria. We meet in what coaches call a 'chemistry session' to check out the potential relationship and our synergy. The other sets will almost certainly have been checked before this clinching interaction when client and professional find out if they gel and can work together.

How we use it

Before choosing someone to work with, we consider each set of criteria to create an ideal profile. We ask:
- How long would we expect this person to have been practising?
- What level of qualification do we expect? From which body?
- What sort of approach would we prefer? For example, Gestalt or TA?
- Are they free when we need them?
- How much do they cost? How would we know they were worth it?
- What sort of approach would work really well for us?

We offer the diagram to clients when they consider possible professional interactions, to help them clarify their needs.

And when we are tendering for work, we also note that all these factors are covered by corporate recruitment processes and so it is useful to audit what someone choosing us would see on each corner!

Elements of Choice

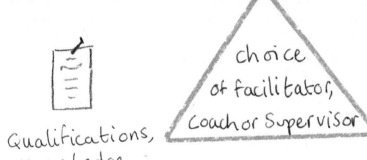
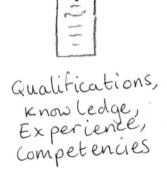

Personal characteristics & Style

choice of facilitator, coach or Supervisor

Qualifications, knowledge, Experience, Competencies

Practical Logistics

Put it into action

If you are prospecting for work, use this model to audit your own profile and to structure how you present it to clients.

If you are looking for someone to do some work with you individually or in a team, for instance a supervisor or someone to run a workshop, ask yourself:

- Which criteria are most important to me? How do they show up?
- Would I travel a long way to work with a very experienced supervisor because I prefer to work in person or can I work by Skype?
- What sort of approach is going to get the team engaged?

The Supervision Cycle

What this is

When a supervisor works with a coach or a facilitator works with a team, they are together reflecting on work that has been done outside the room. Both supervisors and consultants connect regularly and briefly with the client and then part again, hoping that the interaction has value that resonates in their client's world. Learning tends to be multilayered, impacting on self-awareness, professional growth, systems awareness and effective practice.

There is a stage in this model that is about the introduction of new learning. Supervisors, mentors and facilitators appropriately use a wider range of behaviour than coaches. They may share experience and knowledge and give professional guidance in a more directive way. The client will legitimately expect them to have a level of professional expertise that will bring new learning to their practice.

How we use it

We have used this diagram with potential purchasers and clients to develop understanding of the supervision process. We also use it to reflect on our own practice. We ask:
- Are there any aspects of the cycle that we are missing?
- What new learning have we introduced recently?
- How did we do this? What impact did it have?
- What shifts have our clients made?
- How can we support and challenge clients to apply their insights?

Put it into action

Remember that the client alone has responsibility for the *doing*, which is outside the room. Make prompts for each stage of the process and reflect systematically on a client engagement to gain clarity about what has been going on. Then ask:
- What learning do I need myself to resource clients more?

The Supervision Cycle

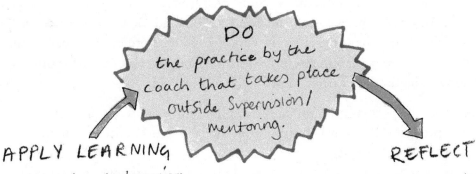

DO the practice by the coach that takes place outside Supervision/mentoring.

REFLECT on practice - experience, relationship, feeling, thoughts, skills - and organisational systems

DISTIL Sift reflection to create new personal & professional insights

INTRODUCE NEW LEARNING Knowledge, models, perspectives from others, competency ladders

SHIFT Reflect on new knowledge & insights. Create new view/model/strategies

APPLY LEARNING to thinking & planning for future practice. Commit to experimentation.

The Supervision Triangle

What this is

This lovely clear model of what supervision covers applies also to what goes on in team coaching and facilitation. Versions of it have been described by Kadushin (1976), Proctor (2000), Hawkins and Smith (2006) and Newton and Napper (2007). It identifies the three areas of work that *must* be present in supervision. We think that they are also present in the often-unspoken contract for other people working in the Learning and Development field.

A supervisor helps us as professionals to explore our work, considering:
- the professional context (norms, professional practice, ethics, systemic and organisational factors)
- our own growth and development (skills and competencies, resources, training, CPD, reading, techniques and tools)
- the emotional impact of our work and the space and support we need to stay appropriately detached from our clients' emotions and needs and their potential impact on us.

The interaction is only supervision when all three aspects of the work are present: partial coverage may be training or a comforting conversation but does not contain all the requirements for safe practice and real professional reflection and growth.

How we use it

We use this model to explain what supervision is. It helps us to clarify the difference between supervision and professional mentoring, especially when we depict mentoring as a circle placed exclusively around the development corner. When we work with groups, we often draw the triangle on a flip chart; ask people to write issues that puzzle or interest them about their work on Post-its and invite them to place these on the appropriate corner of the triangle. This increases understanding of what can usefully be brought to supervision – and what is best reflected on elsewhere.

The Supervision Triangle

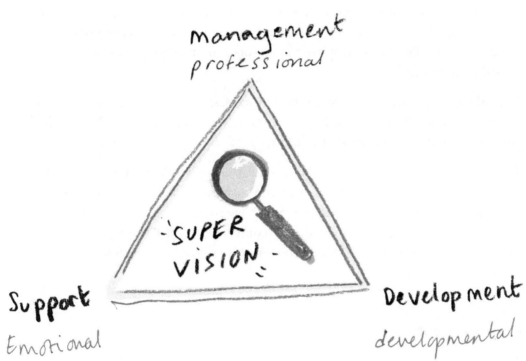

Put it into action

If you want to find support for your own professional development, use the model to:
- help you decide what issues to take to supervision and what to take elsewhere for support
- consider how fully you are using your own supervision
- reflect on which aspect of supervision you are most inclined to seek out and why this might be so.

If you are working to support the learning of others, use the model to:
- distinguish your offer from other interventions
- explain the supervision process.

Making Meaning in Supervision

What this is

In supervision, the coach brings reflections and queries from their practice for exploration with their supervisor in a co-created learning relationship. Enhanced understanding or new meanings are created as coach and supervisor consider the piece together. 'The piece' may be client work, an organisational situation or an ethical conundrum.

In working with a team to explore their processes, a facilitator similarly sits with the team to look at their context and values: what's gone on in work and what's going on in the moment inside the room.

The supervisor sits alongside the client to look at the work within its contexts: organisational, systemic, environmental and relational – hence, the coach and supervisor are side by side in our diagram. New meaning and increased resourcefulness emerge. They are the outcome of the collaborative nature of the work and of its dual focus on phenomenon (case study) and generative environment (context).

How we use it

There are different ways of bringing the case study to the table. They include storytelling, re-enactment, written reflection, witness statements, audio and video recording. Sometimes we listen with supervisees to recordings of their coaching so that we both hear the conversation simultaneously and can share reactions and ideas in the moment.

Put it into action

Use this model with clients to reflect on the mutual enterprise of the work, and the interactive relationship where together you create new awareness for yourselves and for each other. Or use it to focus on the phenomena of your own practice and so strengthen the voice of your own inner supervisor.

Making Meaning in Supervision

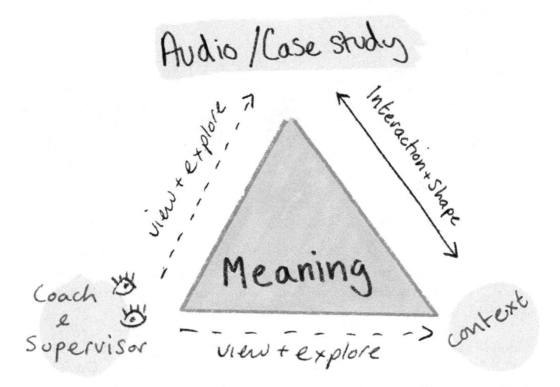

NB 'Coach & supervisor' above could be transposed to other combinations (e.g. team & facilitator, coach & mentor).

The Focus of the Work

What this is

We offer a series of diagrams to clarify the differences between the focuses of coaching, mentoring and supervision, then explain how we use them and how you might put them into action.

The focus of coaching

This simple model appears in Chapter 2. The practitioner works with the client, who is impacted by their world.

The focus of mentoring

The second diagram illustrates how the practitioner, a mentor, works with the client, a coach, focusing on the coach's professional competence. This is often to support accreditation by a professional body. While here the focus is coaching competence, in other fields it will be other areas of competence.

Mentoring has a 'been there, done that' element. A mentor has expertise in the same professional field as the mentee. We can coach rocket scientists (we do!) but we can't mentor them because we have no experience in the area ourselves, so we can't give guidance or advice. On the other hand, when we coach, it can be an advantage to come free of assumptions, as this may lead to questions that cause clients to see their context with fresh eyes.

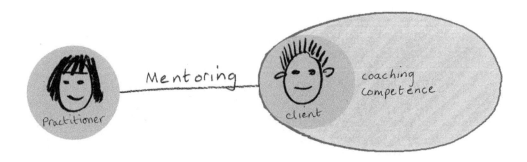

The Focus of Supervision

The third diagram relates to supervision. The practitioner is the supervisor, and the client, or supervisee, is a coach (or another supervisor). The work is focused on the supervisee's practice. Its purpose is to support and develop the supervisee and to keep them and their clients both safe and resourceful. While the supervisor has concern for the supervisee, their focus is also on the wider work of that person and the profession as a whole. The area of the client's practice may include aspects of their personal world as well as their professional world, their clients' personal and professional worlds, and the way all these systems overlap and impact each other.

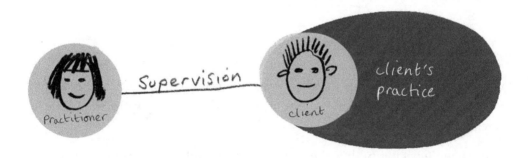

How we use it

These diagrams help us clarify the different perspectives of the interventions, so that we can contract very clearly with the client about the work we are about to do together.

We sometimes explain the differences with the example of a coach who is bereaved. They might seek:

- counselling to work through their grief
- coaching to move forward to new experiences (when ready to do so)
- mentoring to move up the professional competence ladder
- supervision to enquire, 'Am I fit/safe/resourced to coach right now?'

The Focus and the Work

What this is

This composite diagram allows us to see the three interventions, coaching, mentoring and supervision, together. There is an overlap at the centre around the client because we cannot see someone only in one context (i.e. even if the focus of the work is mentoring, we will have some awareness of other aspects, such as the client's personal life, training activities and preferences). We bring who we are to all situations.

Understanding that we may be working in different ways with the same person at different times helps us to clarify and hold the appropriate space for the current piece of work.

How we use it

We hold this diagram in our minds as we make our contract with a client and agree the work, its focus, context, boundaries and desired outcomes, and start to co-create the relationship.

When we are working with a client who is in multiple relationships with someone, we ask them to create a new diagram with relevant labels to help them to explore the boundaries for each type of work and to clarify whether the interventions are mutually incompatible. For instance, in organisations using internal coaching, we might use it with a manager to explore the potential conflict of interest if they set out to coach a direct report.

We also share this model when supervising groups of practitioners who themselves coach and supervise and mentor (and probably do other things, including facilitating, training and consulting). We find it helps people focus on the shifts in practice they make as they move from one type of assignment to another. It offers the space to focus on what falls within each remit and to consider how we may best contract with our client in order to keep the boundaries of the work clear, clean and effective.

The Focus and the Work

Put it into action

These four diagrams are useful for professionals using similar skills in different contexts/roles:

- Use them to explore overlapping yet distinct areas of work.
- Offer them to clients and colleagues to tease out the differences between interventions.
- Use them to check and manage expectations.
- Use a similar model with other potentially overlapping interventions, for example training and facilitation.

Organic Practice

What this is

This model helps individuals and teams understand themselves and each other better. It works for anyone interested in exploring what informs their approaches and behaviour.

Each layer in the triangle is a stratum in our formation. Deep in the base are beliefs we took on years ago. Sometimes, fossilised attitudes and approaches emerge from here and show up in the present. Further up the triangle are other understandings and learnings – a whole range of influences and experiences that shape how we relate to others today.

How we use it

We use the model in supervision to explore the influences on someone's practice. The top of the pyramid represents the approach and style of work we see when that person works with a client or colleague. Underpinning and supporting this visible apex lie all the accumulated learnings, formal and informal, and all the experience, both life and professional, of that practitioner. We invite our supervisees to fill in the layers with things that are pertinent to their own background and then to reflect and discuss how that unique combination might show up in their work.

Put it into action

Use this triangle to explore and articulate your own personal, integrated model of working. Invite others to do so too. Working through it takes you a long way to finding the answer to the question often asked in selection panels, '*What is your model of practice?*'

Feel free to change the names of the layers and their order: we don't mind whether ethics come before beliefs or not! This just stimulates personal exploration.

Organic Practice

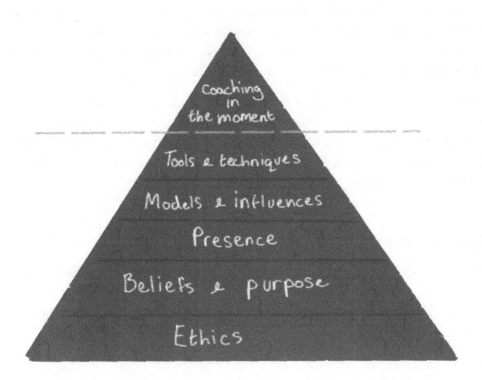

- Take a blank triangle and experiment with it, jotting things down about what has influenced you.
- Consider how deep and how strong each of these influences is, and how near the foundation of your triangle they lie.
- Try out various configurations.
- Share your personal triangle with someone else. Ask them to talk you through it, sensitively exploring how your background shows up in your practice.
- Consider whether you might like to adjust something.
- Bring together what you have discovered in a summary that describes your unique model of practice.
- Follow a similar process with others whom you support.

Team Balloon

What this is

Working with this image helps teams take off and rise to new heights. It is an extended metaphor that facilitates systematic discussion about where a team is heading, what values drive it, how it looks when fulfilling its purpose, what holds it back and what will remove impediments to progress.

The stars and rainbow represent the aspiration of the team – their purpose or mission, and attributes of excellence. The balloon has three horizontal bands – thoughts, language and behaviours. Imagine flames as values to give the balloon lift-off. The basket carries the team. Heavy weights keep it tethered to the ground. Scissors cut the tethers and release it.

How we use it

We explain the metaphor and split the team into small enough groups to allow everyone to participate. Each group has a flip chart to draw and write on. We facilitate discussion to arrive at decisions that gain the support of the whole team.

Put it into action

Use the balloon to help teams clarify their vision, identify their values and work together better. Ask them:

- *Where are you heading?*
- *What will other people see when you get there?*
- *What are the values that inspire you?*
- *If you are to achieve your vision and embody your values, how do you need to think?*
- *If you're thinking like that, what will people hear each other say?*
- *So if this is what people are thinking and saying, how will you be acting towards each other? What specific examples come to mind?*
- *What might hold you back?*
- *What could you do to cut off the weights?*
- *How could you ensure this really happens?*

Team Balloon

Group Differences Matrix

What this is

The most basic form of this diagram is just two intersecting lines. No labels. No scaling. No groups of figures exclaiming at how other people show up or asking them endless questions. As such, it is infinitely adaptable to any type of preference indicator or any way of grouping people into types, for example the Myers–Briggs Type Indicator (MBTI™), which we use here.

The horizontal line represents the Sensing/Intuition dimension; the vertical line the Thinking/Feeling dimension. There is a break in the middle, because preferences are distinct, not on a continuum. The points at the far end of the lines represent a very clear preference. The points near the centre represent a slight preference. The spaces between the lines allow groupings of people who have the two adjacent preferences in their profiles.

How we use it

With a team, we ask people to stand at a point that shows their preference. We use tape and coloured card to mark out the model on the floor. We ask for reflections on the way the team is configured. *What do the various preferences contribute to the team? What gaps might there be? What do they want to ask each other? What might their relative positions explain? What might they like from each other that they are not getting now?*

Working individually with someone who wants to improve communication with colleagues, and who knows their preferences, we use Post-its to represent people. We explore how differences show up and what adjustments in approach might lead to more effective work with others.

Put it into action

If you are working with a team to improve communication:
*   group them according to the combination of letters in their profile
*   ask them to create an advertisement that will appeal to the group in the diametrically opposite space
*   let each group in turn deliver their pitch
*   explore what shifts in approach and language might be useful to the team/company going forward.

Group Differences Matrix

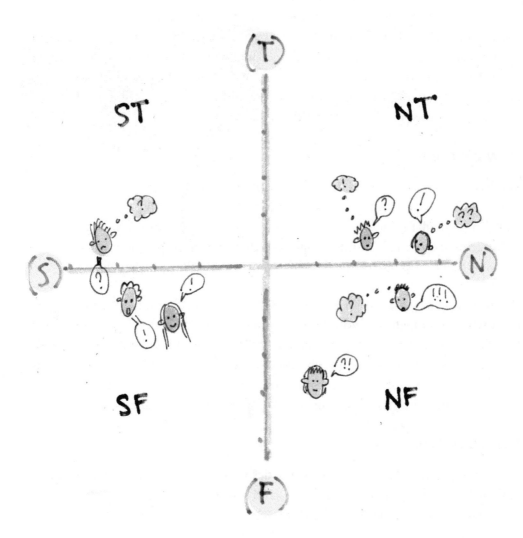

An Even/Uneven Wheel

What this is

This model helps teams reflect on balance in management characteristics, strengths and gaps. The top diagram is a complete wheel: a central hub with circles evenly spaced around it. They all represent characteristics that help a team run smoothly. In an ideal world, every circle would be populated. When any set of characteristics is unrepresented, the circle drops off the wheel, it loses shape and the ride is bumpy. You can adapt the generic wheel to different profiling systems, for example Margerison–McCann or Belbin.

How we use it

We have noticed that when teams recruit new members, they often choose people who are similar to them. This results in lopsided teams, with particular strengths and also particular blind spots. We have used the concept of evenly/unevenly balanced wheels to help teams understand that they need people with a wide range of differing skills and preferences in order to deliver at their best.

We have populated the bottom diagram with a team using nine profiling types of our own. A complete set would be Creator, Instigator, Activator, Continuity Checker, Completer, Reviewer, Tester, Publicist and Networker. They are all necessary in outstanding teams. The Networker is pivotal. This team's wheel is unbalanced, with four people in one group and no one with a preference for three activities. The team has thrust but may lack the ability to evaluate its performance.

Put it into action

Ask the group to identify the characteristics they need across the team to function at their best. Adjust the number of the circles to match. Ask:

- *Who in the team shows the characteristics they need?*
- *What activities are they not drawn towards?*
- *How much are these activities essential to the team?*
- *How are they going to fill the gap?*
- *How are they going to relate to people with different characteristics, who do not seem to fit the prevalent team culture?*
- *How can they connect and value different contributions?*

Even Wheel

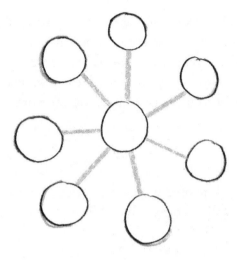

Uneven Wheel

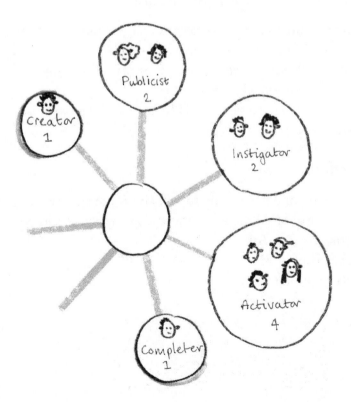

Getting to Win–Win

What this is

This series of pictures, taken from a Quaker peace poster, illustrates the belief that you are more likely to get what you want, or at least some of it, when you cooperate with others than when you fight over resources. As the donkeys strain against each other, both piles of hay are out of reach. Reflecting on the situation, then moving together first to one pile of hay, then the other, allows them both to eat their fill.

How we use it

We use these pictures with people who are worried about conflict at work. We ask them what story the pictures tell and how this relates to what is going on for them:

- *How does this story relate to their habitual response to conflict?*
- *What do other people in the organisation do?*
- *How does this relate to their values?*
- *What are their beliefs about compromise?*
- *What options have they got in the current situation?*

We explore the potential for positive regard that oils joint problem-solving:

- *What strengths do the other people bring to the table?*
- *How could you affirm the positive contributions each of you brings?*
- *What happens when you affirm each other?*
- *What do you need to say about this? Who do you need to say it to? How and when do you need to say it?*

Put it into action

Be mindful that everyone needs time to talk about their needs, to be heard and acknowledged in turn. Hold the space for this to happen. Work with the team on guidelines for the process. Ask:

- *What does everyone need in this situation?*
- *Why do they need this?*
- *Where is the common ground?*
- *What new options for action might there be?*
- *So how could you cooperate?*

Getting to Win–Win

The Team Tree

What this is

This picture offers a way of looking at how individuals perceive their place in the team. It raises questions of relationships, hierarchy, inclusion, succession, threat, enjoyment and engagement. Other diagnostics analyse our contribution to a team or our response in steady state/under stress. They help us understand our colleagues, assemble balanced teams and tolerate each other for the general good. This model explores valuable subjective and emotional perceptions. It helps us identify if the creative type needed to complete the team feels welcome and included, or is just holding on, clinging to the trunk.

How we use it

We use this to develop team understanding, mutual support and more effective ways of working together. People look at the picture and choose the character that most represents how they see themselves in the team. Sometimes we work with people on their own before we work with the team. We may ask people to work in pairs, with a picture each, then in a larger group. We ask:

- *Where do you see yourself? What's it like being there?*
- *Where would you prefer to be?*
- *What might help you change where you are?*
- *What's it like for other people? How could you help others move?*

Put it into action

- Build an atmosphere of trust and openness. Hold this space.
- Give everyone time to identify which character feels most like them and describe what that position feels like.
- Ensure everyone accepts that what someone says is how this person feels . . . not the truth, nor reflection on others, just how they feel.
- Help identify what would help people reach a preferred position.
- Facilitate commitments to support each other.

Team Tree

Chapter 8

Developing Creativity

Creativity

This chapter explores how you can develop your own creativity to work differently with clients and teams.

So far, we have described models we have made and used ourselves. Now is the time for you to experiment!

There is a tantalising tension between urging you to work with people in a uniquely creative way, totally responsive to their needs, and simultaneously offering you pre-prepared models of our own (and other people's). 'Here is one we did earlier' isn't very spontaneous!

However, we use the models we have offered here only as a starting point or stimulus to an individual's exploration of their own situation and responses. We believe that they distil learning. The models that we have created ourselves have been born out of work in the moment with clients. Inspired to find a way to encapsulate a dilemma, query, wondering or pattern, we tentatively offer an outline and almost always the other person adapts it, adds to it, rearranges it or develops it so that they really see a reflection of their own thinking on the page. They almost always want to keep our co-created sketch or model.

The models we create come from synergy: sometimes with each other, more often when we are listening deeply to someone.

Clients give us the stimulus we need to represent what they are describing visually. They offer the spur to drawing by:
- the words they use
- the repeat patterns of words
- the images they employ
- the shapes they make with their hands or map out in the air
- the way they move objects about on a desk.

When we are listening to someone fully, we may notice them, for instance, putting their hands, as it were, at each end of a line that stretches across in front of them. It might be a timeline, or a continuum, or a tug of war between two emotions or ideas. The person has offered us the line! It's up to us to use it to support their exploration.

Here's an example. Years ago, a client was saying repeatedly that he did not want to be arrogant. And yes, we did all the discussion about the evidence and where the belief that he might be arrogant came from. Then as he moved his hands, seeming to stretch a piece of elastic in front of him, we asked, '*What's the opposite of arrogant?*' '*Doormat,*' he replied. And so the arrogant/doormat continuum was born. We drew a line to represent the continuum, and he marked where he was at the time, where else he might have been and where he'd like to be in future. As he looked at this, he was able to explore perception, evidence and a way to develop different behaviours. We also walked along an imaginary arrogant/doormat continuum on the floor and considered the feelings at each point.

Older readers (as they say!) may remember the moon/parrot syndrome of late twentieth-century football. Players interviewed after a match were always 'over the moon' if they had won and 'sick as a parrot' if not. '*How are you doing on the moon/parrot scale?*' still feels like a fun coaching question!

Building on Existing Models

We are confident that you often spot prompts to sharing existing models. When clients talk about changes afoot in their organisation or about struggling with new developments, you may already check whether they are familiar with the Change Curve and explore how they might use it to support their own and their colleagues' process.

The Change Curve is an interesting example of incremental creativity. It has developed over the course of years as different people have refined and added to it. Originating in research on death and dying by Elisabeth Kübler-Ross, it is now widely used to show the stages many of us experience when we face changes in our lives, both personal and professional (see Chapter 6).

Many people already know the Change Curve in one form or another and still have not applied it to their personal situation. As we discuss change and its effects, both personal and systemic, with clients, there is scope to explore more specifically how change is affecting *this* individual, *this* organisation.

Here are some variations on the curve generated in the moment by clients. The drawings come out of discussion about what the client is experiencing and contribute to sense making in new situations. Here's what often happens:

- We hear that there is a change issue.
- We ask about the process.
- Perhaps we ask how this relates to the normal Change Curve.
- The client draws how it feels for them right now/how they see other people responding to the change that's going on.
- We explore where the drawings take us.

Put it into action

Consider which other models you know that lend themselves to being personalised in this way in the moment with the client. Then experiment.

Variations on the Change Curve

The ripples of change through an organisation

Board   Exec   Staff

Change churn

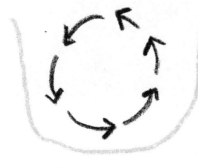

Variations on the Organic Practice Model

Recently, we used our Organic Practice model (see Chapter 7) in a workshop. A couple of months later, one of the participants approached us saying she had adapted it and asked permission to use the extended model with her colleagues and teams. We were delighted. Models give us a framework for exploring ideas and concepts. They stimulate creativity and new thinking. They must develop constantly to support reflective practice. Here's her adapted model:

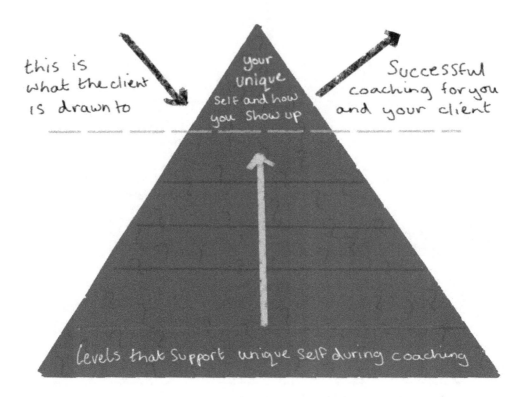

Interacting with and adding to a diagram stimulates our thinking. We make new connections and see synergy. Personalised models speak powerfully to their creators and offer new insights to others.

Our drawings and diagrams are work in progress, thinking in visible action. This chapter is about you experimenting, sharing and taking wing.

Spotting the Triggers

The Hand Dance

People sketch their life and understanding all around them as they speak. They may present:

- a timeline with past and future at different points – watch out for the hand gesture and movement usually across the front of the body, occasionally behind and in front of the speaker
- mood swings, low and higher hand movements
- binary choices: hands gesturing in turn; on the one hand . . . on the other hand
- hand near heart, on stomach, clutching throat
- their approach to or feelings about people or situations: chopping movements, vague waving, pointing and cutting forward.

Our response can start with simply mirroring the gesture and a gentle question: 'What's *this*?' Fascinatingly, people can almost always tell us what the gesture means, even though they don't consciously know when they are making it. We can then work with it for powerful effect.

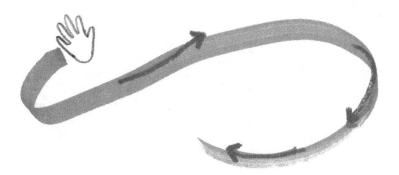

Put it into action

Take this forward into creating images with clients of what they are mapping in space with their hands. Sketch the shape out as you say, '*I can see a shape like this emerging*' '*How does that look?*' '*What's going on?*' Expect your client to seize the pen and take over. Follow the trail.

Linguistic Clues: In their Own Words

Clients show us their reference points and internal landscape in their speech. Language is littered with images, similes and metaphors. Our role as coaches is to notice the patterns that are unique to the speaker. Our personal language patterns, our *idiolect*, is as unique to us as our fingerprint and gives identity almost as clearly.

A coaching client talked repeatedly about her frustration with herself as '*Like a dog chasing a stick.*' After a few more conventional questions, we asked, '*What would you do if you were a cat?*' This precipitated a huge creative breakthrough about possible actions. For this client, a drawing of a cat could be a positive reminder and spur to action in the future.

Another client was going through a sticky time at work and had lost self-confidence. He felt under scrutiny and disabled. We asked him what it would look like if he drew how he felt at the moment. He drew a filing cabinet.

We explored what he would like to be instead. The conversation opened up areas such as autonomy, respectful relationships, trust, personal values, external judgements and internal validation. We asked what he would like to be instead of a filing cabinet. He said a molecular structure. We asked how this might look.

He drew the diagram below, with nodes to represent key aspects that would enable him to be the person he wanted to be.

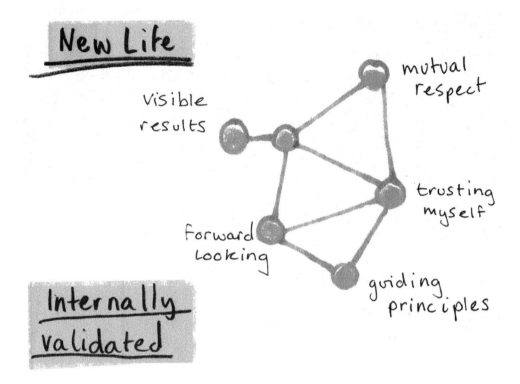

A third client talked about having lost all fire for life. We asked what it would look like if she had internal fire. She drew a flame, using soft blues and purples in a sinuous pattern and overwriting the picture with the values she wanted to personify and live by.

Put it into action

Give time to the client to create drawings such as this. The act of drawing is also an act of discovery.

Respect and Celebrate the Client's Choice

It could be tempting to hear clues such as the ones we have described above and to think, '*Ah, that's it; we need to draw a cat/dog/ship/flame.*' We find that in practice, most clients do give potent clues to how they would visually represent an idea through the language they use. However, they may make another choice.

Recently, a client talked about his work situation: he mentioned his crew and the organisation being '*all at sea*'. He told us that he felt a bit '*out of his depth*' and over an hour or so we heard about '*washed up*', '*all hands on deck*' and '*lifelines*'. These were a few words among thousands: we speak at about 110–150 words per minute. So the theme here was not ludicrously obvious. However, when we picked up on the language and used it back, the client felt heard and understood his state more clearly. He wanted to consider what and who he wanted in the *lifeboat* with him. Then he mapped this out. Not in a drawing, which might have been our choice, but in a sort of grid, which was his choice. The exploration of metaphor aided his thinking, which he was then able to systematise in a grid that he could return to and use for reference as he went forward.

Put it into action

Notice the prompts – then let the client choose how to use them to create something supportive in their own way.

Shapes for Thinking

Circles

Traditionally, the circle is the perfect shape: equal, smooth and without end or beginning. A ring, the symbol of marriage, is used in many logos. The five interlocking Olympic rings denote interconnection and continuity.

We may have strong positive associations with circles, or may think more readily about vicious circles and endless repetition. We need to watch out for the client's perspective, so that the model suits the emotional response.

A client talked about pressures at work that made her feel unsafe. Drawing her in a circle of safety, with arrows representing pressures from outside and ways of keeping boundaries in place, enabled her to externalise the emotions, reduce the panic and gather resourcefulness for the future.

Put it into action

Remember that the circle has several interesting relations – loop, spiral, wheel, cycle, oval, pie and Venn. Listen out for linguistic clues about what would fit someone's thinking. If a client says, '*I am going round in circles*' ask, '*What's the circle like?*' or '*Could you draw the circle?*'

When you hear a repeating process, try capturing it visually. A client might say, '*I tell her the figures for the month; she gets angry; I become upset and go off and hide and see if I can change anything. Then next month I dread giving the figures and so leave it late. She gets angry again.*' Turn this into a cycle! Get the client to draw it and ask them at which points they might choose to break the cycle.

Triangles and Pyramids

Some triangles sit strongly on their base, rising in rarefied layers to point onward and upward. Others offer three equal ingredients and show the optimum mix. Three is a most beguiling number, the magic number! One is just one; two may be a coincidence; three is a pattern; and by four we begin to be bored with repetition. So we have three wishes, three witches, three bears and tripartite meetings to set up coaching. We also, of course, have the eternal triangle!

Models evolve through conversation. As we work together, and interact with a model, our ideas develop and new layers of meaning open up. Making Meaning in Supervision (page 166) is an example of a triangle evolving:

1 We talked about the co-created learning environment in supervision: how together we explore meaning. We remembered a triangular literary theory model that places reader and author at the same point.
2 We thought about how supervisor and supervisee sit alongside each other in an equal developmental relationship and adapted the literary theory model to show this.
3 Jenny shared the model with a group who refined it more.

Put it into action

Experiment with a triangle when:
- you are exploring layers of influence or development
- someone is talking about what is fundamental or foundational
- three factors are balanced in some way
- three elements are needed to create a viable whole
- three things are in tension or competition.

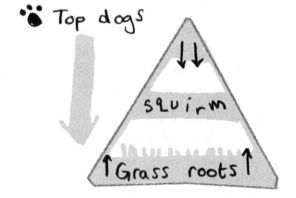

Squares – and Boxes

Neat, tidy, containing and somehow square – but thinking inside a series of boxes can help us think out of the box!

Matrices made up of square or rectangular arrangements in rows and columns help us represent:

- mixes of factors – e.g. urgent/important
- movement from one state to another – e.g. situational leadership
- relationship between similar things – e.g. positioning your practice.

A grid can be useful to compare different aspects of the whole (e.g. Strengths, Weaknesses, Opportunities, Threats (SWOT)), allowing comfortable space to write in the boxes expanding the content. We can also mark out grids on the floor and walk from one space to another, savouring the experience in each area – good for gaining different perspectives and for kinaesthetic processors.

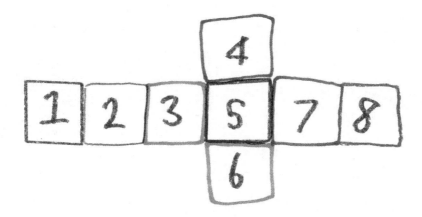

Put it into action

Watch out for the square being too like 'ticking the box' or too confining. There's a danger that when we have filled a box with ideas, we believe we have no more to offer and the exercise is complete. A contained space is no good for brainstorming – so allow the boundaries of the square to flex.

Lines

Lines have a bit of a bad press. When did you last hear someone say 'linear' as a compliment? But lines and their variants have a place in creative work. A line may be straight, curvy, stepped, continuous, broken, arrowed, dotted.

The line as a continuum between two extremes offers possibilities for clients to move along it testing out responses to different points. When you hear someone talking about polarised positions, there is scope for exploration and mapping the continuum out together on paper or in space.

A lifeline is another form of linear work. This is not palmistry! It's an invitation to consider how we understand our experience and progress to date and what stories we tell ourselves and others about that. The lifeline may be any shape and may have illustrations, notes, arrows, mnemonics, Post-its or collage along the way.

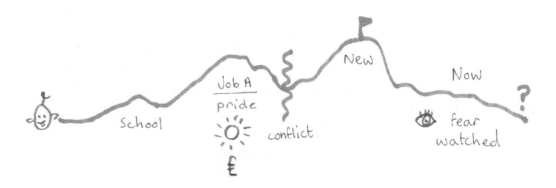

Put it into action

Watch out for someone mapping a timeline, or a potential balance line (on the one hand/on the other) with their hands. This is a great trigger to offer them paper to spread out and capture more of what they are saying by drawing and writing. Help them harness their own, perhaps unnoticed, creativity to allow them to see more of themselves.

If you are drawing a lifeline with a client, use lots of space and time and allow for emotional responses. Consider the scope of the lifeline. Is it about the whole of life so far? Or does it focus on career or a specific aspect of life?

Drawing Freely in the Moment

And then there are pictures such as the team tree or donkeys, or the girl with the balloons below. A client created this drawing for herself as a prompt to let go of tasks she was holding unnecessarily. She was holding on to them because of other people's expectations, not because she had decided herself that they were essential. She was motivated by the '*shoulds*' and '*oughts*' of others. She continues to use this picture as a visual reminder of her commitment to herself.

This image came out of a session with a client who kept on trying the same solution to a rocky problem and kept on walking splat into it. We imagined what it would be like to reach his desired outcome and then looked back at the rock from the other side and created a path round it. This was a co-created drawing – the client added lots of detail in words and pictures to give life to the path around the rock, and took the picture away.

One client said a situation was like being at the bottom of a deep pit and not being able to get out. We asked, '*What would it be like if you had a ladder?*' and sketched the pit and the ladder. The client then started describing the rungs of the ladder and the way out. This moved the client from a space of despairing stuckness to a resourceful state, where she could see the first steps to take.

The sort of situation we have drawn below happens to lots of clients. They get caught in the middle of a multitude of tensions, responsibilities in different directions and messages about what they should do, transmitted through different layers of the hierarchy. It's an agonising place to be, and you can often lose sight of what's created the tension because the experience of the moment is so intense. Drawing this helped a client to realise why he was under pressure and to separate out the various lines of communication that he could influence in different ways to improve his sense of control and sanity.

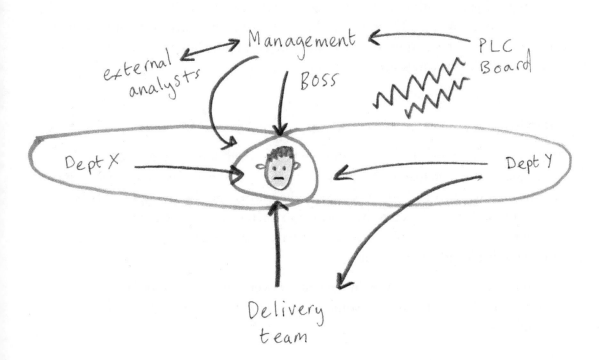

To Draw or Not to Draw?

Seeing the client

Coaches sometimes assume that this work can only be done face to face. We believe that the whole range of different interventions can be used effectively whether or not we are physically present with the client. Even if we can't see the client, we can say, '*That sounds like a repeated cycle to me*' or '*How are you seeing it?*' or '*How might you see the stages of that pattern?*'

We have done on the phone almost every type of work we do face to face: drawing, mapping with objects, moving the body to denote different responses, walking a line, taking different physical perspectives. The work is about widening the way the client sees things and need not be constrained by whether or not we see them or the drawings that they produce.

Sensitivities

We notice that most clients, even those who, if asked directly, might say they can't draw, will sketch and map things out to develop their ideas and expand their options. However, there are some times when it may not be appropriate to use these approaches. We need to be sensitive to clients' states, preferences and current capacity. We should balance sensitivity with enough appropriate challenge to stretch ideas and comfort zone.

We might be wary of this work if a client was very emotional, though using it appropriately could lead us to some content free work that might be very helpful.

And finally . . .

Don't look at me in that tone of voice, it smells a funny colour!

This old saying shows how our responses to things mix media and senses. We (and our clients) use all our senses to process and understand the world. Our role is to help them learn from themselves across the whole gamut of their experience.

And Always Finish with a Review . . .

What are you taking with you from this book:
* in your bag of learning?
* in your feelings?
* in your thoughts?
* as you walk into the future?

Chapter 9

References and Further Reading

References and Further Reading

Many models in this book are original to Jenny Bird and Sarah Gornall, for instance all the models in Chapter 2. The illustrations were created by Josie Vallely based on diagrams by the authors.

This chapter contains:
- some background information
- references where we have mentioned other published works
- options for reading further if you would like to follow up on ideas, theory or research.

It is arranged by order of the models, to give you sources for the ideas or diagrams that we have reproduced or adapted. Often our work does not draw on a particular publication, but there may be a related body of knowledge that you may wish to explore further. We've suggested some titles, though these are an indication of where you might like to start, rather than an exhaustive reading list.

Chapter 1: Introduction

Neuroscience

Neuroscience is the scientific study of the nervous system, though many of us think of it as the study of the brain and how it influences our behaviour. In one sense, neuroscience is immensely old; think ancient Egypt and trepanning. In another sense, it is very modern and the pace of advance in the field has increased phenomenally in recent years. Many coaches think neuroscience offers scientific validation for techniques that they have used effectively in their own practice. The founding fathers (and they do seem to be almost entirely men) of the 1950s and 1960s scoped and explored the area that has now become modern neuroscience. The first free-standing department of neuroscience opened at Harvard Medical School in 1966.

Several recent texts describe how coaches and other professionals can use our default patterns and preferences to support clients' learning and achievement aims.

Brann, A. (2013) *Make Your Brain Work*. London: Kogan Page.

Brown, P. and Brown, V. (2012) *Neuropsychology for Coaches*. Maidenhead: Oxford University Press.

Rock, D. (2009) *Your Brain at Work*. New York: HarperCollins.

Chapter 2: Coaching

The Coaching Process

There are lots of books about how to coach, some of which we reference here. Myles Downey's *Effective Coaching* is one of the seminal ones, as is Timothy Gallwey's *Inner Game* series. We refer to other useful books, such as John Whitmore's *Coaching for Performance*, at other points in this chapter.

The websites of the three main professional coaching associations in the UK are also very useful sources of reference. They detail professional codes of ethics and describe coaching competencies.

Downey, M. (1999) *Effective Coaching*. London: Texere.

Gallwey, T. (1975) *The Inner Game of Tennis*. London: Pan Macmillan.

Gallwey, T. (2000) *The Inner Game of Work*. New York: Random House.

Kline, N. (1999) *Time to Think*. London: Ward Lock.

Lee, G. (2003) *Leadership Coaching*. London: CIPD.

McMahon, G. and Archer, A. (2010) *101 Coaching Strategies and Techniques*. London: Routledge.

Rogers, J. (2004) *Coaching Skills: A Handbook*. Maidenhead: Oxford University Press.

International Coach Federation (ICF) www.coachfederation.org and www.coachfederation.org.uk

European Mentoring and Coaching Council (EMCC) www.emccouncil.org and www.emccuk.org

Association for Coaching (AC) www.associationforcoaching.com

Making Meaning in Coaching

Literary theory refers in the most basic sense to the systematic study of literature and of the methods for studying and analysing literature. More interestingly perhaps, it includes the view that meaning is made anew as each new reader reads the text. Many of our approaches in this book and in coaching have much in common with the idea that meaning is dependent on perspective, experience, culture, belief systems, etc. So some of our models spring from literary theories about the juxtaposition of reader and writer or about the plurality of texts.

We notice an interesting parallel process here. We are referring to literary theory in a book about coaching because of our own perspective or background, probably not one hugely common to coaches. So the lens we bring to coaching is from another part of our world view. You might even spot, from the dates of the recommended reading, when we studied this!

Belsey, C. (1980) *Critical Practice*. London: Methuen.

Eagleton, T. (1983) *Literary Theory*. Oxford: Basil Blackwell.

Chapter 3: Relationships and Communication

Communication Model

Communication theory is another branch of study emerging in the twentieth century: it is a mix of maths, information research and human psychology. Alan Turing, credited with breaking the Enigma code in the Second World War, is probably now the best-known exponent of a branch of this work in the UK. Claude Shannon (1916–2001), a seminal thinker in the field of communication studies, wrote, '*The fundamental problem of communication is that of reproducing at one point either exactly or approximately a message selected at another point.*'

As this area of study grew, it changed from being entirely focused on the technical means of communication to include human and psychological influences and interference.

Fiske, J. (1990) *An Introduction to Communication Studies*. London: Routledge.

Weaver, W. and Shannon, C. E. (1963) *The Mathematical Theory of Communication*. Champaign, IL: University of Illinois Press.

Communication Pie

We mention that what people most want from their leaders is honesty. This assertion is based on the work of Jim Kouzes and Barry Posner, who have researched leadership qualities for over thirty years.

Kouzes, J. and Posner, B. (2008) *The Leadership Challenge* (4th edn). San Francisco, CA: Jossey-Bass.

Mehrabian, A. (1971) *Silent Messages*. Belmont, CA: Wadsworth.

Interactional Triangle

We make a reference here to 'an imago'. Tactile models or imagos are used in many disciplines to promote learning and understanding of our own mental pictures. Coaches, therapists and other professionals may on occasion use a variety of visual and tactile representations to allow a client to model or mirror a situation or perception. For a tactile imago, the professional may provide a number of items for the client to arrange to describe a situation: these could be almost any collection of small things – stones or pebbles, shells, nuts and bolts, or little plastic figures. The client arranges these in juxtaposition in order to describe what is happening in a group or organisation.

Tactile imagos share with sculpting and constellations work the advantage that we can move items around in order to develop our ideas and understanding. This is potentially more dynamic than a diagram.

Work using actual people to represent a situation or organisational structure may be a sculpt where people are placed in positions and contact with each other like a living sculpture. Constellation work will often allow one person to place volunteers (perhaps the rest of a group) in different places, possibly joining them by having each hold a rope or ribbon in connection with others.

All these methods allow the client to create a version of a complex system and stand outside it to consider different perspectives, their own connections with others and the juxtapositions, both existing and ideal, of the various players.

Cochrane, H. and Newton, T. (2011) *Supervision for Coaches*. Ipswich: Supervision for Coaches.

Whittington, J. (2012) *Systemic Coaching and Constellations: An Introduction to the Principles, Practices and Application*. London: Kogan Page.

Iceberg

The metaphor of the iceberg as a model of the human mind was first used by Sigmund Freud (1856–1939), the founder of psychoanalysis. He started experimenting with the 'talking cure' in the late 1880s. In his model, the unconscious is a greater part than the conscious. When clients present with negative or undesired patterns of behaviour, the elements of the iceberg below the water are at play.

Anna Freud, who is less in the public mind than her father, also did important early work on psychology, developing the concept of the ego setting up defences to keep the self from pain.

Freud, A. (1948) *The Ego and the Mechanisms of Defence*. London: The Hogarth Press.

Freud, S. (1990) *The Interpretation of Dreams* (trans. Joyce Crick). Oxford: Oxford University Press.

Johari Window

Hanson, P. (1973) 'The Johari Window: A Model for Soliciting and Giving Feedback', in Jones, J. and Pfeiffer, J. W. (eds) *The 1973 Annual Handbook for Facilitators*. San Diego, CA: Pfeiffer & Company.

Luft, J. (1970) *Group Processes: An Introduction to Group Dynamics* (2nd edn). Palo Alto, CA: National Press Books.

Peltier, B. (2001) *The Psychology of Executive Coaching*. Abingdon: Routledge.

Emotional Intelligence Cone

The theory that there are multiple forms or presentations of intelligence was proposed, controversially, by Howard Gardner in the 1980s. This is a hotly debated area, now overshadowed by new findings in neuroscience. However, the models of emotional and social intelligence, which are helpful in the work of changing communications and relational behaviour, build on the idea that there are interpersonal and intrapersonal (Gardner's terms) aspects of intelligence.

Gardner, H. (1983) *Frames of Mind: The Theory of Multiple Intelligences*. London: Fontana.

Goleman, D. (1995) *Emotional Intelligence*. New York: Bantam Books.

Goleman, D. (2006) *Social Intelligence*. New York: Hutchinson.

Drama and Winners' Triangles

Transactional Analysis, or TA, lies within the humanist tradition of psychology and originated in the work of Eric Berne. It gives us frameworks for understanding what is going on both internally and interpersonally and why it is going on like it is. The underlying philosophy of TA is that people are OK –

that is, they have worth and integrity as human beings, and they have the capacity to think, make decisions about their own destiny and change those decisions. TA brings us the concepts of scripts, life positions and ego-states, as well as the Drama and Winners' Triangles. Some of the terminology of TA has now become part of everyday language, without people being conscious of the origin of the ideas they are drawing on.

Scripts are written at an early age and determine many of the decisions we make. As adults, we can become aware of these scripts and choose to rewrite them. Coaching may help us to do this.

Each of the three ego-states, parent, adult and child, is a bundle of attitudes, patterns of thinking and fixed points of view. Each ego-state has both a positive intention for us and potentially a negative aspect. Sometimes we forget about the positive intention!

Life positions are evaluations about ourselves or others. They unconsciously or consciously inform our decisions and justify our behaviour. Simply raising awareness about the life position that a client is holding will help to open up new possibilities.

Berne, E. (1964) *Games People Play: The Psychology of Human Relationships*. London: Penguin.

Choy, A. (1990) 'The Winners' Triangle', *Transactional Analysis Journal*, 20(1).

Harris, T. (1969) *I'm OK, You're OK: A Practical Guide to Transactional Analysis*. New York: Harper & Row.

Hay, J. (1993) *Working It Out at Work*. Watford: Sherwood.

Karpman, S. (1968) 'Fairy Tales and Script Drama analysis', *Transactional Analysis Journal*, 7(26).

Napper, R. and Newton, T. (2000) *Tactics*. Ipswich: TA Resources.

Stewart, I. and Joines, V. (1987) *TA Today*. Nottingham: Lifespan.

International TA Association (ITTA) www.itaaworld.org

UK Association for Transactional Analysis (UKATA) www.uktransactionalanalysis.co.uk

Chapter 4: Learning and Personal Growth

Experiential Learning Cycle

Honey, P. and Mumford, A. (1982) *Manual of Learning Styles*. London: Peter Honey.

Kolb, D. (1984) *Experiential Learning: Experience as the Source of Learning and Development*. Upper Saddle River, NJ: Prentice Hall.

Cycles in Psychological Models

Coaching has its roots in a body of psychological knowledge that is constantly developing our understanding of the human mind. Using psychological models can help coaches to illuminate the thinking, feelings, desires and reasoning that influence a client's decisions and actions, and this can lead to attitudinal shift and transformational change. Using a psychodynamic model (i.e. exploring the way the mind, emotions, personality and motivations interact) is an approach that descends directly from the work of Sigmund Freud (see above).

Aaron Beck and Albert Ellis were also hugely influential in developing ideas that have become widely accepted now, though they were revelatory at the time. The branch of psychology that developed from their work, cognitive psychology, explores the way the mind creates patterns of thinking and internal dialogue in response to external stimuli. The language used internally shapes a person's map of reality and influences emotions and actions. Working analytically to gain awareness of patterns of language is often the first step in uncovering the chain of assumptions and beliefs from which behaviour springs. Once a particular cycle is broken open, a fresh one can be constructed.

If you would like to read more, here are some books that give a brief introduction to the field. *The Complete Handbook of Coaching* has a short introductory chapter on a range of psychological approaches to coaching, with more detailed further reading lists for each approach. *50 Psychology Classics* gives a brief overview of major psychological traditions through describing the work of a seminal writer in each case.

Beck, A. (1976) *Cognitive Therapy and the Emotional Disorders*. New York: Grove Press.

Briers, S. (2009) *Brilliant Cognitive Behavioural Therapy*. Harlow: Pearson.

Butler-Bowdon, T. (2007) *50 Psychology Classics*. London: Nicholas Brealey.

Cox, E., Bachkirova, T. and Clutterbuck, D. (eds) (2010) *The Complete Handbook of Coaching*. London: SAGE.

Ellis, A. and Harper, R. (1975) *A New Guide to Rational Living*. Englewood Cliffs, NJ: Prentice Hall.

Hough, M. (1994) *A Practical Approach to Counselling*. Harlow: Longman.

Competence Ladder

The term 'conscious competence' was almost undoubtedly coined in the USA in relation to progression of skills as a teacher or learner. If you want to find out in detail, you could explore the www.businessballs.com website, which has the full text of a 1969 article by Martin Broadwell about teaching skills, which mentions the 'third level, the Conscious Competent', and a 1974 article by W. Lewis Robinson entitled 'Conscious Competency: The Mark of a Competent Instructor'.

It is widely accepted that four stages of learning, *unconsciously unskilled*, *consciously unskilled*, *consciously skilled* and *unconsciously skilled*, were described in manuals developed by the American training organisation Gordon Training International in the 1970s.

Dilts' Neurological Levels

Neuro-Linguistic Programming (NLP) originates from the work of Richard Bandler and John Grinder, working in the USA in the 1970s. It brings together ideas from a number of disciplines, including psychotherapy, linguistics and hypnotherapy, and offers practical exercises for changing the way we see the world, talk about our involvement within it and act.

Neuro relates to the nervous system and the sensory filters through which we perceive the world (sight, hearing, touch, taste and smell). *Linguistic* relates to the language we use to organise our beliefs, our interpretation of the world and how we communicate with other people. *Programming* relates to our habits of thought, feelings and action. The premise of NLP is that we have the potential to change this programming.

Phrases such as '*The map is not the territory*' and '*There is no failure, only feedback*' come from NLP. Beliefs commonly associated with NLP include:

- Every behaviour has a positive intent.
- People have all the inner resources they need to succeed.
- You are in charge of your mind and therefore of your results.

NLP techniques include using modelling, anchoring, metaphor, eye-accessing cues and logical levels. Our version of Dilts' Logical Levels is based on the original model, which was developed by Robert Dilts and Todd Epstein. The underlying concept connects with the work of anthropologist Gregory Bateson and philosopher Bertrand Russell on logical types.

Adler, H. (1994) *NLP: The New Art and Science of Getting What You Want.* London: Piatkus.

Bandler, R. and Grinder, J. (1975/1976) *The Structure of Magic: A Book about Language and Therapy* (Vols 1 & 2). Palo Alto, CA: Science & Behavior Books.

Bateson, G. (1972) *Steps to an Ecology of Mind.* Chicago, IL: University of Chicago Press.

Dilts, R. (1990) *Changing Belief Systems with NLP.* Capitol, CA: Meta Publications.

Ready, R. and Burton, K. (2004) *Neuro-Linguistic Programming for Dummies.* Chichester: John Wiley.

Chapter 5: Leading, Influencing and Motivating

Circles of Leadership

Adair, J. (1987) *Effective Teambuilding.* London: Pan Books.

The Leadership Journey

There are, of course, many theories about leadership and what differentiates good managers from good leaders. Two twenty-first-century writers whose work is influencing the way people think about leadership are William Torbert and Jim Collins.

Torbert counters the widely held assumption that leaders are born, not made, proposing instead that leaders are made, not born. He suggests that leaders who undertake a journey of personal growth and understanding can further develop their personality and extend their repertoire, with a transformational impact for themselves and their companies. He identifies seven different styles of response, or action logics – opportunist, diplomat, expert, achiever, individualist, strategist and alchemist – and sees progression through these as a developmental pathway that leads to greater and greater effectiveness. Those who reach the ultimate stage, the alchemists, just one per cent of the group profiled for Torbert's research, are not only effective as transformational leaders, but are also able to generate society-wide change.

Collins has looked at what moves companies from being good companies to great companies, and concludes that it is essential to have great people at all levels of the organisation. As individuals (Level 1), team members (Level 2), managers (Level 3), leaders (Level 4) and executives (Level 5), they need to be the best they can be in the role they hold and to act with a sense of disciplined responsibility. To transform their companies from good to great, Level 5 Leaders need all the attributes that have made them successful at earlier stages in their career – knowledge, talent, skills, effective teamworking, organisational ability, results orientation and vision – and also a blend of personal humility and intense professional determination.

Collins, J. (2001) *Good to Great*. New York: HarperCollins.

Rooke, R. and Torbert, W. R. (2005) 'Seven Transformations of Leadership', *Harvard Business Review*, April.

Contextual Leadership

Goleman, D. (2002) *Primal Leadership: Realizing the Power of Emotional Intelligence*. Boston, MA: Harvard Business School Press.

Leadership Style, Skill and Will

Hersey, P. and Blanchard, K. (1982) *Situational Leadership: A Summary*. San Diego, CA: University Associates.

Hierarchies of Need

The early work on hierarchies of needs was done by Abraham Maslow. He proposed the concept in his 1943 paper 'A Theory of Human Motivation'. Maslow described the layers of need without offering a visual representation. The theory has been much adapted, much debated and much described, so that multiple models (sometimes contradictory) are available through search engines and sharing websites. Maslow's original hierarchy had five layers, and these have been expanded, explained and added to by later commentators and theorists in various disciplines, including John Whitmore, who related the model to a coaching culture.

Maslow, A. H. (1943) 'A Theory of Human Motivation', *Psychological Review*, 50: 370–96, available at: http://psychoclassics.yorku.ca (accessed 25 January 2015).

Maslow, A. H. (1954) *Motivation and Personality*. New York: Harper.

Whitmore, J. (1992) *Coaching for Performance*. London: Nicholas Brealey.

Levels of Consultation and Decision Making

Writing in the 1960s, against a background of a rising desire for greater public involvement in decisions that had a bearing on the organisation of society, Sherry Arnstein addressed the issue of citizen power, or citizen participation, which she described as '*the redistribution of power that enables the have-not citizens, presently excluded from the political and economic processes, to be deliberately included in the future.*'

Arnstein identified eight levels of participation, which went like this: Level 1 – manipulation; Level 2 – therapy; Level 3 – informing; Level 4 – consultation; Level 5 – placation; Level 6 – partnership; Level 7 – delegated power; Level 8 – citizen control. She classed Levels 1 and 2 as Non-Participation, Levels 3–5 as Tokenism and only Levels 6–8 as Citizen Power. The thinking behind her analysis, which she expands on in terms of our wider society and public services, is transferable to aspects of corporate organisation and staff engagement. Her seminal article is freely available online. It was reprinted in *The City Reader*, cited below.

Arnstein, S. R. (1969) 'A Ladder of Citizen Participation', *Journal of the American Institute of Planners (JAIP)*, 35(4), available at: www.planning.org/ (accessed 25 January 2015).

Gates, R. and Stout, F. (1996) *The City Reader*. New York: Routledge.

Support Challenge Matrix

The idea that everyone needs a balance of both challenge and support in order to learn and grow was put forward by Nevitt Sanford, a professor of psychology at the University of California, who was sacked for refusing to sign the loyalty oath in 1950. He did research at the Tavistock Institute in London, returned to the States and had a distinguished academic career, publishing research into higher education. Alongside the concept of growth being fostered by appropriate challenge and appropriate support, Sanford later wrote about the concept of readiness to grow – both challenge and support must come at the appropriate time.

In this book, we use a matrix to help clients develop their ability to challenge and support their teams. The ability to be appropriately challenging and supportive in our coaching is important as well. There is sometimes a view in the corporate world that coaching is the soft fluffy stuff. If it is, it won't succeed. The need for iron as well as compassion is explored in more detail in *Executive Coaching with Backbone and Heart* and *Challenging Coaching*, cited below.

Blakey, J. and Day, I. (2012) *Challenging Coaching*. London: Nicholas Brealey.

O'Neill, M. B. (2000) *Executive Coaching with Backbone and Heart*. San Francisco, CA: Jossey-Bass.

Sanford, N. (1962) *The American College*. New York: Wiley.

Chapter 6: Analysis, Choice and Change

Mapping our Thinking

Tony Buzan popularised using radial diagrams to map information in the 1970s, both on television and in his book *Use Your Head*. While people have used graphics as a way of generating and organising ideas over the centuries, Buzan's guidelines have helped countless students develop their study skills.

Buzan, T. (1974) *Use Your Head*. London: Ariel Books.

The Balance Wheel

The wheel, symbolising wholeness of life, seems to originate from Buddhism. Legend has it that the *Bhavacakra* (Sanskrit), the first representation of the wheel of life, was created by the Buddha himself to explain complex teachings in a simple form. It presents the cycles of existence. We were touched to find that Elisabeth Kübler-Ross titled her *Memoir of Living and Dying* 'The Wheel of Life', referring, we believe, to the many metaphors about cycles of life and the seasons that abound in many cultures.

Using a visual of a wheel is widespread in coaching practice. In general in coaching, it is used as a scaling tool exploring an individual's level of satisfaction with different areas of life. There may be other applications where it appears as a more prescriptive pattern of what a balanced life might contain. In coaching texts, there are many examples of varying wheels, adapted for clients or circumstances.

Gornall, S. and Burn, M. (2013) *Coaching and Learning in Schools: A Practical Guide.* London: SAGE.

Whitworth, L., Kimsey-House, H. and Sandahl, P. (1998) *Co-Active Coaching.* Palo Alto, CA: Davies-Black.

Do-It Disc

We understand that President Eisenhower gave a speech at an Assembly of the World Council of Churches in 1954 in which he quoted a college principal as saying, '*I have two kinds of problems, the urgent and the important. The urgent are not important, and the important are never urgent.*' This has been re-quoted in various forms. The underlying principle underpins popular time management matrices. One of these has been described in detail by Stephen Covey.

Covey, S. R. (1989) *The 7 Habits of Highly Effective People.* London: Simon & Schuster.

Tracy, B. (2004) *Eat That Frog.* London: Hodder & Stoughton.

Quote Investigator http://quoteinvestigator.com/2014/05/09/urgent/ (accessed 27 January 2015).

SWOT

SWOT is essentially a brainstorming instrument that helps lay the conditions for new thinking and ideas (see *lateral thinking* below). We first came across it as a leadership tool for analysis and planning well over twenty years ago when we worked in executive teams. A number of websites describe ways of using a SWOT analysis and different views of the origins of the SWOT model. These include a detailed history on www.businessballs.com of how the model emerged in the 1960s through work at the Stanford Research Institute, with Albert S. Humphrey credited as 'one of the founding fathers'. However, Wikipedia, that fount of learning and knowledge, says that 'Humphrey himself does not claim the creation of SWOT, and the origins remain obscure.'

Force Field Analysis

Force Field Analysis originates from the work of Kurt Lewin, an American social psychologist, associated with 'Gestalt' psychology. Gestalt works with the idea that the mind tries to make a complete picture out of what is by its nature something in flux. Organisations, life, our personalities, are forever changing or merging into a new state. Yet we try to capture the here and now and interpret it as though it is an immutable truth. The 'field' we are in is dynamic and changes with time and experience, as we interact internally with external stimuli. The external forces may be positive or negative, weak or strong. The balance (or not) of those forces has impact on personal and organisational development. If an organisation wants to move towards change, Lewin suggests that the most effective first step is to reduce the negative forces that are restraining progress.

Lewin, K. (1943) 'Defining the "Field at a Given Time"', *Psychological Review*, 50: 292–310. Republished (1997) in *Resolving Social Conflicts & Field Theory in Social Science*. Washington, DC: American Psychological Association.

The Change Process

Almost all the leaders we work with are familiar with a version of the Change Curve. Indeed, the people we coach have usually been on the receiving end of what has been known since around the 1990s as 'Change Management'.

There are numerous versions and variations of the Change Curve available, each with different patterns of dip and peak and with varying words for the suggested stages of the process.

Ideas about how people notice and accept change (in the form of innovation) may first have been explored by Everett Rogers in the 1960s. He offered the groupings of people accepting new inventions or situations as: Innovators, Early Adopters, Early Majority, Late Majority and Laggards.

Everett Rogers' ideas seem to have fused with Elisabeth Kübler-Ross' concept of stages of grief in the field of change management, starting perhaps with a paper by McKinsey consultant Julien Phillips in the early 1980s. After years of working with the dying and their families, Kübler-Ross described five phases of grief. Drawing on this, the change curves that are frequently used in business today posit the idea of movement (not necessarily linear or predictable) through a range of emotional responses. A major factor in the idea of the change process is that the aim is to finish at an improved (in some sense for the organisation) state of existence: perhaps more streamlined, more profitable, more competitive or more technically current. Not just to return to equilibrium. All this depends, of course, on whether the change is internally instigated or forced by external factors.

Kübler-Ross, E. (1989) *On Death and Dying*. London: Routledge.

Phillips, J. R. (1983) 'Enhancing the Effectiveness of Organizational Change Management', *Human Resource Management*, 22(1/2): 183–99.

Rogers, E. M. (1962) *Diffusion of Innovations*. Glencoe: Free Press.

Change Analysis

Lateral thinking as a term is sometimes counterposed with 'vertical thinking'. When we think in a linear way, we tend to follow a logical analytical trail, building one step or statement squarely on the foundation of the previous one. Traditional educational approaches emphasise the development of this sort of logic, which is beneficial in many situations. However, it does not always serve the development of new ideas, as our thinking may be contained within the boundaries of the route we have embarked on, or may trip up over logical objections.

Edward de Bono opened out a new way of thinking, of accessing insights and thinking 'outside the box', with his work in the 1960s. The term 'lateral thinking' is his. He suggests ways of bypassing the logical route, starting from different points of view and working with analogy and metaphor to challenge assumptions and generate ideas. This sort of creative thinking is not boundaried by concepts of 'correctness'. It can help people access intuition and different ways of knowing and put together information from a variety of disparate sources together in fresh, interesting and potentially productive ways.

Techniques used to stimulate lateral thinking include brainstorming, reverse brainstorming ('*Let's think of everything we could do to make this a terrible place to work in*') and working systematically from different perspectives, as in the *Six Thinking Hats* exercise.

de Bono, E. (1970) *Lateral Thinking: Creativity Step by Step*. New York: Harper & Row.

de Bono, E. (2000) *Six Thinking Hats*. London: Penguin Books.

Chapter 7: Supervision and Team Facilitation

Supervision

The information we give in this chapter about supervision and its function in supporting coaches to practise effectively, safely and resourcefully, builds on descriptions of coaching in Chapter 2.

Supervision for coaches is increasingly a prerequisite for commissioning organisations, and it is defined, described and encouraged (if not yet formally required) by the coaching professional bodies. So there are many similar definitions of coaching supervision to be found on the relevant websites. For example, the Association of Coaching Supervisors states: '*Supervision on a 1-1 or group basis is the formal opportunity for coaches working with clients to share, in confidence, their case load activity to gain insight, support and direction for themselves, thereby enabling them to better work in the service of their clients.*'

Carroll, M. and Gilbert, M. C. (2005) *On Being a Supervisee*. London: Vukani.

Cochrane, H. and Newton, T. (2011) *Supervision for Coaches*. Ipswich: Supervision for Coaches.

Hay, J. (2007) *Reflective Practice and Supervision for Coaches*. Maidenhead: Oxford University Press.

Murdoch, E. and Arnold, J. (eds) (2013) *Full Spectrum Supervision*. St Albans: Panoma Press.

Association of Coaching Supervisors (AoCS) www.associationofcoachingsupervisors.com

International Coach Federation (ICF) www.coachfederation.org

European Mentoring and Coaching Council (EMCC) www.emccouncil.org

Association for Coaching (AC) www.associationforcoaching.com

The Supervision Triangle

The Supervision Triangle diagram appears for the first time in the article in the *TA Journal* in 2007 cited below. It is a model of the balance of the functions of supervision. The functions have been described in different ways over time, and the evolution of the triangle is well described in Cochrane and Newton's work *Supervision for Coaches*, cited above.

Hawkins, P. and Smith, N. (2006) *Coaching Mentoring and Organizational Consultancy*. Maidenhead: Oxford University Press.

Kadushin, A. (1976) *Supervision in Social Work*. New York: Columbia University.

Newton, T. and Napper, R. (2007) 'The Bigger Picture: Supervision as an Educational Framework for All Fields', *Transactional Analysis Journal*, 37(2).

Proctor, B. (2000) *Group Supervision: A Guide to Creative Practice*. London: SAGE.

Group Differences Matrix

The Myers–Briggs Type Indicator (MBTI) is an instrument for helping people gain a clearer understanding of themselves and the way they interact with others. Companies often use MBTI profiling for leaders and teams with the aim of improving self-awareness and team dynamics. The instrument draws on Carl Jung's work on psychological types in the 1920s and was developed by a mother-and-daughter team, Katherine Briggs and Isabel Briggs Myers.

The MBTI questionnaire helps to identify preferences in four different aspects of your personality. The pairs of preferences are:
*   Extraversion or Introversion (E or I) – relating to where you prefer to get and focus your energy
*   Sensing or Intuition (S or N) – relating to the kind of information you prefer to gather and trust
*   Thinking or Feeling (T or F) – relating to the process you prefer to use when you make decisions
*   Judging or Perceiving (J or P) – relating to how you prefer to deal with the world around you.

People's types are expressed as combinations of one letter from each aspect, for example ENTP. There are 16 different combinations, some with a higher representation among certain professional groups.

Briggs Myers, I. with Myers, P. (1995) *Gifts Differing: Understanding Personality Types*. Palo Alto, CA: Davies-Black.

Jung, C. G. (1971) *Psychological Types*. Oxford: Harcourt, Brace.

Kiersey, D. (1998) *Please Understand Me*. Delmar: Prometheus Nemesis.

An Even/Uneven Wheel

Different teams perform differently. People within them react to each other differently. Yet those joining a team often assume that the other members of the team will react in the same way that they do. Understanding difference can help individuals to adapt and the team to function better.

Studying team dynamics in the 1970s led Meredith Belbin to propose that people tend to behave, contribute and interrelate with others in particular ways, which he then grouped and described as 'roles'. Having described eight roles initially, Belbin re-categorised some and added a ninth in 1988. The roles are now called Plant, Resource Investigator, Coordinator, Shaper, Monitor-Evaluator, Teamworker, Implementer, Completer-Finisher and Specialist. Belbin's work has been widely used to support team development.

Two Australians, Charles Margerison and Dick McCann, developed another instrument for measuring the effectiveness of teams through looking at balance across the team. The underpinning research identifies nine different success factors – Advising, Innovating, Promoting, Developing, Organising, Producing, Inspecting, Maintaining and Linking – and related roles that team members typically play. Each brings benefit to the team and organisation. The work is described well online.

Belbin, R. M. (1981) *Management Teams: Why They Succeed or Fail*. Oxford: Butterworth-Heinemann.

Leadership Interview with Margerison and McCann (2 June 2012) www.leadershipforwomen.com.au (website of the Australian Centre for Leadership for Women).

Getting to Win–Win

Our illustration of two mules is based on a cartoon entitled *Cooperation is Better than Conflict*, produced by the Friends (Quakers) Peace Committee, in 1933. The design may originally have been sketched out by John Hunter, a member of the committee, but there is no record of this. The cartoon was used on posters and also featured for a while as the cover illustration for a book that used fairy tales to help readers realise that conflict is not always a bad thing, but can release creative energy and give birth to new ideas, and that everyone can be an agent of change.

Leimdorfer, T. (1992) *Once Upon a Conflict: Fairy Tale Manual of Conflict Resolution for All Ages*. London: Quaker Peace & Service.

Chapter 8: Creativity

Our clients' models

The following diagrams were originally created by clients and redrawn with their permission:

- Organic Coaching Model Plus
- Filing Cabinet and the Molecules
- Balloon Woman.

Index

action logics 215
action-centred leadership model 98
Adair, John 98, 214
Adler, H. 214
analysis 124–45; and balance wheel 130–1,
    217–8; developmental wheel 136–7; do-it
    disc 138–9, 218; force-field analysis 144–5,
    219; review pentagon 140–1; scaled wheel
    132–3; SWOT 142–3, 197, 218; Venn
    diagrams 128–9; wheel of work 134–5
Archer, A. 207
Arnold, J. 221
Arnstein, Sherry 114, 216
arrogant/doormat continuum 187
Association of Coaching Supervisors (AoCS)
    221
Association for Coaching (AC) 207, 221
axis of ego 118–19

Bachkirova, T. 213
baggage 30–1
balance wheel 130–1, 217–18; scaled
    132–3
balloon woman picture 199
Bandler, Richard 213–14
Bateson, Gregory 214
Beck, Aaron 212
Belbin, Meredith 178, 223
Belsey, C. 208
Berne, Eric 210–11
Blakey, J. 217
Blanchard, K. 110, 215
body language 42–4
boxes 197

brainstorming 144, 197, 218, 220
Brann, A. 206
Briers, S. 212
Briggs, Katherine 222
Briggs Myers, Isabel 222
Broadwell, Martin 213
Brown, P. 206
Brown, V. 206
Buddhism 217
Burn, M. 218
burn out 54,134
Burton, K. 214
Butler-Bowdon, T. 213
Buzan, Tony 126, 217

Carroll, M. 221
change 124–55, 217–20; and transition slice
    148–9
change analysis 152–3, 220
change curve 188–90, 219; variations on
    190
change process 150–1, 219–20
chemistry sessions 30
choice 124; choosing a facilitator, coach or
    supervisor 160
Choy, A. 60, 211
circles: of leadership 98–9, 215; of safety 195;
    shape for thinking 195; vicious 80–1
citizen participation, Arnstein's ladder of 114,
    216
climbing the mountain 154–5
Clutterbuck, D. 213
co-operation 180–1, 223
coach persona 26–7

coaching; focus of 24–5, 168, 170–1; making meaning in 22–3, 207–8; organic coaching model 172–3, 190
coaching contract *see* contract/contracting
coaching series 20–1
coaching session 16–17
coaching space 28–9
coaching style of leadership 108
Cochrane, H. 209, 221
cognitive psychology 212
Collins, Jim 104, 214–5
comfort zone 86, 86–9
communication 38–65; model of 40–1, 208
communication pie 42–3, 208
compass 116–17
competence ladder 84–5, 213
conscious competence 84–5, 213
consultation, levels of 114–15, 216
contextual leadership 108–9, 215
contract/contracting 16; levels of the 32–3; organisational 32; sticking with the 18–19; three-way 32
Covey, Stephen 218
Cox, E. 213
creativity 185–203; building on existing models 188–90; and change curve 188–9, 219; drawing freely in the moment 199–201; linguistic clues 192–4; shapes for thinking 195–201; spotting the triggers 191–4
cycle, supervision 162–3
cycles in psychological models 74–9, 212–13; negative 76, 77; neutral 76, 79; positive 76, 78

Day, I. 217
de Bono, Edward 152, 220
decision making, levels of 114–15, 216
developmental wheel 136–7
dialogic process, coaching as 28
Dilts' neurological levels 90–1, 106, 213–14
do-it disc 138–9, 218
donkey picture 180–1, 223
Downey, Myles 207

drama triangle 54–9, 210–11
drawing freely in the moment 199–201

Eagleton, T. 208
ego, axis of 118–19
ego states 211
Eisenhower, D. D. 138, 218
Ellis, Albert 212–13
emotional intelligence cone 52–3, 210
energy, maximised 100–1
European Mentoring and Coaching Council (EMCC) 207, 221
even/uneven wheel 178–9, 223
experiential learning cycle 72–3, 212

feedback 50, 140
Fiske, J. 208
focus: of coaching 24–5, 168, 170–1; of mentoring 168, 170–1; of supervision 169, 170–1
force field analysis 144–5, 219
Freud, Anna 210
Freud, Sigmund 48, 209–10, 212
futures-based planning 146–7

Gallwey, Timothy 207
Gardner, Howard 210
Gates, R. 216
Gestalt psychology 219
Gilbert, M. 221
goals 20–1, 136
Goleman, Daniel 52, 108, 210, 215
Gordon Training International 213
Gornall, S. 218
grids 197
Grinder, John 213–14
group differences matrix 176–7, 222
group work 159
groups 158–9

hand dance 191
Harris, T. 211
Hawkins, P. 222
Hay, J. 211, 221

Hersey, P. 110, 215
hierarchies of need 112–13, 215–16
Honey, Peter 72, 212
Hough, M. 213
Humphrey, Albert S. 218
Hunter, John 223

iceberg 48–9, 209
idiolect 192
imago 46, 209
influence, spheres of 102–3
Ingham, Harrington 50
intelligence, emotional 52–3, 210
interactional triangle 46–7, 209
internal responses 44–5
International Coach Federation (ICF) 207, 221
International TA Association (ITTA) 211

Johari window 50–1, 210
Joines, V. 211
Jones, J. 210
Jung, Carl 222

Kadushin, A. 164, 222
Karpman, K. 54, 211
Kiersey, D. 222
Kimsey-House, H. 218
Kline, N. 207
Kolb, David 72, 212
Kouzes, J. 208
Kübler-Ross, Elizabeth 150, 188, 217, 219–20

ladder: of citizen participation 114, 216; competence 84–5, 213
language 42–3, 192–4
lateral thinking 220
leadership 96–121; action-centred model 98; circles of 98–9; coaching style of 108; contextual 108–9, 215; levels of consultation and decision making 114–15, 216; and maximised energy 100–1; neurological levels for management style

106–7; situational 110; and support challenge matrix 120–1, 216–17
leadership journey 104–5, 214–15
leadership style, skill and will 110–11, 215
learning 68–93; comfort, stretch, panic zones in 86–9; and competence ladder 84–5, 213; Dilts' neurological levels 90–1, 106, 213–14; strengths smiley 92–3
learning cycle 70–1; experiential 72–3, 212
learning economy 68
Lee, G. 207
Leimdorfer, T. 223
Lewin, Kurt 219
life positions 211
lifeline 198
lines 198
linguistic clues 192–4, 195
literary theory 196, 207–8
Luft, Joseph 50, 210

McCann, Dick 178, 223
McMahon, G. 207
management style, neurological levels for 106–7
mapping our thinking 126–7, 217
Margerison, Charles 178, 223
Maslow, Abraham 112, 215–16
matrix (matrices) 197; group differences 176–7, 222; support challenge 120–1, 216–17
maximised energy 100–1
meaning: making of in coaching 22–3, 207–8; making of in supervision 166–7, 196
meeting, tripartite 34–5
Mehrabian, Albert 42, 208
mentoring 24, 164; focus of 168, 170–1; mentoring as a leadership style 110–11
mind maps 126, 217
models, building on existing 188–90
moon/parrot syndrome 187
motivation: and hierarchies of need 112, 215–16; and support challenge matrix 120–1, 216–17

mountain, climbing the 154–5
Mumford, Alan 72, 212
Murdoch, M. 221
Myers–Briggs Type Indicator (MBTI) 176–7,
    222
Myers, P. 222

Napper, R. 54, 60, 164, 211, 222
need, hierarchies of 112–13, 215–16
negative cycles 76–7
neuro-linguistic programming (NLP)
    213–14
neurological levels, Dilts' 90–1, 106,
    213–14
neurological levels for management style
    106–7
neuroscience 68, 90, 206
neutral cycles 76, 79
new life drawing (filing cabinet and
    molecules) 192–3
Newton, T. 54, 60, 164, 209, 221–2

O'Neill, M.B. 217
organic practice 172–3, 190
organisational contract 32

panic zone 86, 86–9
Peltier, Bruce 50, 210
pentagon, review 140–1
perception, client's 24, 74
persecutor role 55, 58, 60
personal growth 68–93
Pfeiffer, J.W. 210
Phillips, Julien 219–20
pit and ladder drawing 200
Plan-Do-Review 70
planning, futures-based 146–7
positive cycles 76, 78
Posner, B. 208
preconscious 48
prioritising tasks: and do-it disc 138–9,
    218
proactive, being 61, 62, 64

Proctor, B. 164, 222
progress, monitoring of: and climbing a
    mountain 154–5
psychological models, cycles in 74–9,
    212–13
pyramids 196; pyramid of needs 113

Quaker peace poster 180–1, 223

Ready, R. 214
reflection 14–15,18, 163
relationships 38–65; and drama triangle 54–9,
    210–11; and emotional intelligence cone
    52–3, 210; interactional triangle 46–7,
    209; and Johari window 50–1; and
    winners' triangle 54, 60–5, 210–11
rescuer role 54, 55, 57, 60
responsible, being 61, 62, 63
review pentagon 140–1
review process 20, 203
Robinson, W. Lewis 213
rock picture 200
Rock, David 5, 206
Rogers, Everett 219–20
Rogers, J. 207
Rooke, R. 215

safety, circle of 195
Sandahl, P. 218
Sanford, Nevitt 216–17
scaled balance wheel 132–3
self-esteem, boosting of 92
self talk, negative/positive/neutral 76–9
sensitivity 202
Shannon, Claude Elwood 40, 208
shapes for thinking 195–201; circles 195;
    lines 198; squares/boxes 197; triangles and
    pyramids 196
situational leadership 110
Six Thinking Hats 152, 220
smiley, strengths 92–3
Smith, N. 222
spidergrams 126
spirals, virtuous 80–1

spheres of influence 102–3
squares 197
stars and clouds 82–3
Stewart, I. 211
Stout, R. 216
strengths smiley 92–3
stretch zone 86–9
styles of leadership 108–11, 215
supervision 24, 158–73, 196, 221; focus of
    169, 170–1; making meaning in 166–7,
    196; and organic practice 172–3, 190
supervision cycle 162–3
supervision triangle 164–5, 221–2
support challenge matrix 120–1, 216–17
SWOT 142–3, 197, 218
synergy 186

tactile imagos 46, 209
team balloon 174–5
team building 52, 159
team facilitation 158, 159
team tree 182–3, 199
teams 158–9; even/uneven wheel 178–9,
    223; getting to win-win 180–1, 223; and
    group differences matrix 176–7, 222
tension drawing 201
thinking: mapping our 126–7, 217; shapes for
    see shapes for thinking
third-party coaching 24
three-way contract 32
timeline 198
Torbert, William 104, 214–15
Tracy, B. 218
transactional analysis (TA) 210–11

transition slice 148–9
triangle(s): drama 54–9, 210–11; interactional
    46–7, 209; shapes for thinking 196;
    supervision 164–5, 221–2; and winners'
    triangle 54, 60–5, 210–11
tripartite meeting 34–5
true north 116–17
Turing, Alan 208

UK Association for Transactional Analysis
    (UKATA) 211
unconscious 48, 50, 209
unconscious competence/incompetence
    84–5, 213

Venn diagrams 98, 128–9; invented 128–9
Venn, John 128
vicious circles 80–1
victim role 55, 59, 60
virtuous spirals 80–1
voice tone 42–3, 44
voicing 61, 62, 65

Weaver, Warren 40, 208
wheel: balance 130–1, 217–18;
    developmental 136–7; even/uneven
    178–9, 223; scaled balance 132–3
wheel of life 130–3
wheel of work 134–5
Whittington, J. 209
Whitmore, John 112, 207, 216
Whitworth, L. 218
win-win, getting to 180–1, 223
winners' triangle 54, 60–5, 210–11